A full refutation of the doctrine of unconditional perseverance: in a discourse on Hebrews, Chapter ii. Verse 3. ... By Thomas Olivers.

Thomas Olivers

A full refutation of the doctrine of unconditional perseverance: in a discourse on Hebrews, Chapter ii. Verse 3. ... By Thomas Olivers.
Olivers, Thomas
ESTCID: T116827
Reproduction from British Library
With a final advertisement leaf.
London : printed by R. Hawes: and sold by J. Parsons; at New Chapel, City Road, and by the booksellers in town and country, 1790.
ix,[1],191,[3]p. ; 12°

Eighteenth Century
Collections Online
Print Editions

Gale ECCO Print Editions

Relive history with *Eighteenth Century Collections Online*, now available in print for the independent historian and collector. This series includes the most significant English-language and foreign-language works printed in Great Britain during the eighteenth century, and is organized in seven different subject areas including literature and language; medicine, science, and technology; and religion and philosophy. The collection also includes thousands of important works from the Americas.

The eighteenth century has been called "The Age of Enlightenment." It was a period of rapid advance in print culture and publishing, in world exploration, and in the rapid growth of science and technology – all of which had a profound impact on the political and cultural landscape. At the end of the century the American Revolution, French Revolution and Industrial Revolution, perhaps three of the most significant events in modern history, set in motion developments that eventually dominated world political, economic, and social life.

In a groundbreaking effort, Gale initiated a revolution of its own: digitization of epic proportions to preserve these invaluable works in the largest online archive of its kind. Contributions from major world libraries constitute over 175,000 original printed works. Scanned images of the actual pages, rather than transcriptions, recreate the works ***as they first appeared.***

Now for the first time, these high-quality digital scans of original works are available via print-on-demand, making them readily accessible to libraries, students, independent scholars, and readers of all ages.

For our initial release we have created seven robust collections to form one the world's most comprehensive catalogs of 18th century works.

Initial Gale ECCO Print Editions collections include:

History and Geography
Rich in titles on English life and social history, this collection spans the world as it was known to eighteenth-century historians and explorers. Titles include a wealth of travel accounts and diaries, histories of nations from throughout the world, and maps and charts of a world that was still being discovered. Students of the War of American Independence will find fascinating accounts from the British side of conflict.

Social Science

Delve into what it was like to live during the eighteenth century by reading the first-hand accounts of everyday people, including city dwellers and farmers, businessmen and bankers, artisans and merchants, artists and their patrons, politicians and their constituents. Original texts make the American, French, and Industrial revolutions vividly contemporary.

Medicine, Science and Technology

Medical theory and practice of the 1700s developed rapidly, as is evidenced by the extensive collection, which includes descriptions of diseases, their conditions, and treatments. Books on science and technology, agriculture, military technology, natural philosophy, even cookbooks, are all contained here.

Literature and Language

Western literary study flows out of eighteenth-century works by Alexander Pope, Daniel Defoe, Henry Fielding, Frances Burney, Denis Diderot, Johann Gottfried Herder, Johann Wolfgang von Goethe, and others. Experience the birth of the modern novel, or compare the development of language using dictionaries and grammar discourses.

Religion and Philosophy

The Age of Enlightenment profoundly enriched religious and philosophical understanding and continues to influence present-day thinking. Works collected here include masterpieces by David Hume, Immanuel Kant, and Jean-Jacques Rousseau, as well as religious sermons and moral debates on the issues of the day, such as the slave trade. The Age of Reason saw conflict between Protestantism and Catholicism transformed into one between faith and logic -- a debate that continues in the twenty-first century.

Law and Reference

This collection reveals the history of English common law and Empire law in a vastly changing world of British expansion. Dominating the legal field is the *Commentaries of the Law of England* by Sir William Blackstone, which first appeared in 1765. Reference works such as almanacs and catalogues continue to educate us by revealing the day-to-day workings of society.

Fine Arts

The eighteenth-century fascination with Greek and Roman antiquity followed the systematic excavation of the ruins at Pompeii and Herculaneum in southern Italy; and after 1750 a neoclassical style dominated all artistic fields. The titles here trace developments in mostly English-language works on painting, sculpture, architecture, music, theater, and other disciplines. Instructional works on musical instruments, catalogs of art objects, comic operas, and more are also included.

The BiblioLife Network

This project was made possible in part by the BiblioLife Network (BLN), a project aimed at addressing some of the huge challenges facing book preservationists around the world. The BLN includes libraries, library networks, archives, subject matter experts, online communities and library service providers. We believe every book ever published should be available as a high-quality print reproduction; printed on-demand anywhere in the world. This insures the ongoing accessibility of the content and helps generate sustainable revenue for the libraries and organizations that work to preserve these important materials.

The following book is in the "public domain" and represents an authentic reproduction of the text as printed by the original publisher. While we have attempted to accurately maintain the integrity of the original work, there are sometimes problems with the original work or the micro-film from which the books were digitized. This can result in minor errors in reproduction. Possible imperfections include missing and blurred pages, poor pictures, markings and other reproduction issues beyond our control. Because this work is culturally important, we have made it available as part of our commitment to protecting, preserving, and promoting the world's literature.

GUIDE TO FOLD-OUTS MAPS and OVERSIZED IMAGES

The book you are reading was digitized from microfilm captured over the past thirty to forty years. Years after the creation of the original microfilm, the book was converted to digital files and made available in an online database.

In an online database, page images do not need to conform to the size restrictions found in a printed book. When converting these images back into a printed bound book, the page sizes are standardized in ways that maintain the detail of the original. For large images, such as fold-out maps, the original page image is split into two or more pages

Guidelines used to determine how to split the page image follows:

- Some images are split vertically; large images require vertical and horizontal splits.
- For horizontal splits, the content is split left to right.
- For vertical splits, the content is split from top to bottom.
- For both vertical and horizontal splits, the image is processed from top left to bottom right.

John Bickersley

A FULL
REFUTATION
OF THE
DOCTRINE
OF
UNCONDITIONAL PERSEVERANCE:
IN A
DISCOURSE
ON
HEBREWS, Chapter ii. Verse 3.

IN WHICH THE POSSIBILITY AND DANGER OF
THE TOTAL AND FINAL APOSTACY OF TRUE
BELIEVERS IS DEMONSTRATED AND THE
EPISTLE TO THE HEBREWS IS SHEWN TO BE NO
OTHER THAN A REGULAR TREATISE, OR
ONE CONNECTED CHAIN OF REASONING ON
THAT SUBJECT.

By THOMAS OLIVERS.

TAKE HEED, BRETHREN, LEST THERE BE IN ANY
OF YOU AN EVIL HEART OF UNBELIEF, IN DE-
PARTING FROM THE LIVING GOD.
PAUL to the Heb.

BE NOT CARRIED AWAY WITH DIVERS AND STRANGE
DOCTRINES, FOR IT IS A GOOD THING THAT
THE HEART BE ESTABLISHED WITH GRACE
Ibid

LONDON:
PRINTED BY R. HAWES, QUEEN STREET, MOORFIELDS
And sold by J. Parsons, Bookseller, No 21, Pater noster Row, at
the New Chapel, City Road, and by the Booksellers in
Town and Country. MDCCXC.

A PREFATORY DEDICATION:

TO THE REVEREND *JOHN WESLEY*, A.M.

Late Fellow of Lincoln College, Oxford.

Sir,

AS GOD has made you the First Instrument in the present revival of Religion in these lands, whereby so many thousands have been turned from the evil of their way; as you have laboured, in carrying on this work, for the long space of upwards of Sixty years, and with a degree of zeal, diligence, and fortitude, unknown since the days of the apostles; and as you still continue your mighty labours, without the leaft abatement, though you are now in the Eighty-Eighth (or as fome fay, in the Ninetieth) year of your age! and efpecially, as you have always been the great Patron of every doctrine of Univerfal Grace, and, among the reft, of that maintained in the following pages; on all thefe accounts I beg leave, Sir, to recommend this work to your favour and protection, in preference to that of any other. And I farther beg your acceptance thereof, as another (and perhaps the laft) proof of my real affection for your perfon, and alfo, of the very high efteem I hope ever to entertain of your very extraordinary character.

However unworthy the Performance may be, the Subject, Sir, is capable of great fervice to the caufe of Truth, as it ftands oppofed to the popular, and growing error of *unconditional Perfeverance*.

verance. For if it be fully demonstrated, that *that* doctrine is no Truth of Revelation, then it will follow that the doctrine of *unconditional Election* has no foundation in Scripture; from whence it will follow farther, that the doctrine which supposes all things to be unconditionally decreed from eternity, is an unscriptural error. therefore, if the pillar of unconditional perseverance is fairly pulled away, the whole temple of this Dagon comes down of course.

Now the argument, which I have urged in the following pages, does this infallibly. For there, Sir, you will find it demonstrated, that one of the most excellent books of the New Testament, is no other than a regular chain of reasoning against the doctrine of unconditional perseverance. And that I may prevent all clamour, and make the argument the more decisive, at least, with those in this day, who see more force in the SAYINGS of their admired authors, than in a number of the most perfect demonstrations; to confute and silence, if not to convince these, I have confirmed my interpretation of those passages on which I rest a great part of my proof, with the Testimonies of a great number, both of Calvinists and Arminians: whom I largely shew to agree with me in my account of the SCOPE of the whole epistle.

In doing this, I confess I have not paid any regard to what the calvinian writers OUGHT to have said on their own supposition, nor unto what they HAVE ACTUALLY said on various other occasions. It is enough for me, when I say that such words or phrases signify APOSTASY, TOTAL, or FINAL apostasy, that I can find a sufficient number of calvinian writers who say the same; when this is done, no one can expect
me

me to be refponfible for the abfurdities, and contradictions, with which they fo generally abound.

As to the Method, I beg leave to obferve, Sir, that the Difcourfe was originally an extemporary fermon, on the words cited in the beginning; and that when I was prevailed on to enlarge the fubject, and fit it for the reception of the public, I refolved to fpare myfelf the trouble of laying down a new plan; the confequence is, that the argument is rather more complex than the fubject neceffarily requires; feeing, according to this, it would have been fufficient to have fhewn, firft, that thefe Hebrews were true believers; and, fecondly, that, notwithftanding this, they were capable of total and final apoftafy.

However, Sir, there is one circumftance which in all likelihood you will deem a peculiarity, if not an excellency: that as my bufinefs lies folely in the
epiftle

epistle to the Hebrews, I have confined myself very closely unto it. For, first, though there are a great number of propositions most fully demonstrated, there is not so much as a single demonstration brought out of any other part of the Bible. Nor, secondly, is any other part thereof made use of above twice or thrice, either in introducing, illustrating, or amplifying any one point in the whole tract; except when I have been obliged to turn to the Old Testament, in explaining a few passages which the apostle has quoted from thence.

Thus, Sir, I have given you a full account of this small affair—But before I conclude, I must intreat you not to expect any thing great or excellent on the occasion. No, Sir, I do not, I dare not make any pretence to deep learning, or great abilities. For the very

very utmoſt I pretend to is, a ſmall degree of zeal; employing a little common ſenſe; which call to their aid a few ſhreds of learning; to aſſiſt Truth to ſtand its ground againſt a moſt dreadful and dangerous Error.

That you may yet continue here, as a Star of the firſt magnitude, in the right hand of Him who walketh in the midſt of the Golden Candleſticks, and be as the brightneſs of the Firmament, and as the Stars for ever and ever, is,

Reverend Sir,

the Prayer of

your dutiful Son,

and Servant,

THOMAS OLIVERS.

A FULL REFUTATION, &c.

Hebrews, ii. 3.

HOW SHALL WE ESCAPE, IF WE NEGLECT SO GREAT SALVATION?

SALVATION—the Neglect of it—the Consequence of that neglect—and the impossibility of escaping that consequence, are the awful particulars contained in this passage. It is therefore of deep and universal importance that this subject be well understood, by all who profess the name of Christ.

But is this the case? Do all who profess his name, understand it in any tolerable degree? Do they know what the apostle means by *Salvation?* and what by *neglecting* it? I am confident they do not: and

I greatly fear that this is the case, not of Professors only; but even of some who are Teachers of our holy religion.

The common way of explaining these words is, to represent this great Salvation as signifying actual deliverance from sin and hell; that to *neglect* it signifies, not to seek and embrace it; and that this is done, only by careless, impenitent unbelievers: all which is as contrary to the intent of the apostle, and the scope of the whole epistle, as light is to darkness, or as Heaven is to Hell.

One reason why many mistake the true meaning of particular passages of Scripture, is, they adopt systems which are incompatible with Truth; and to prevent their giving up a favourite hypothesis, find themselves under the necessity of inventing such interpretations as will agree with their own schemes; which is the case in the passage now under consideration: by which means the lovely face of Truth is quite concealed, and error, in a thousand forms, appears in its stead.

Some

Some also, who maintain the Truth in general, fall into great mistakes on particular passages, for want of considering the text in close connexion with its context. This is certainly necessary in order to a right understanding of any passage; but more especially if the terms, on which the greatest stress is laid, are equivocal or ambiguous. Now this is the case in the passage before us. The terms Salvation, and Neglect are equivocal; and therefore their meaning can only be ascertained by a strict attention to the connexion of the place, and the scope of the whole epistle.

This, therefore, I shall be careful to do: to consider the words, only as a link of that chain of which the whole epistle consists. In doing which I shall attend to the OCCASION and DESIGN of the epistle, and, as far as I shall judge it necessary, to the apostle's manner of reasoning therein.

By these means I shall be able to shew,

I. What we are to understand, by so GREAT SALVATION.

II. What by NEGLECTING it. And,

III.

III. The CONSEQUENCE of so doing, and the impossibility of escaping that consequence.

IV. I shall then, in the fourth place, conclude with an inference or two.

I. And, first, I am to shew, what we are to understand by, so great Salvation.

The term Salvation, as used in scripture, is, in general to be understood strictly and properly, according to its grammatical import. In this sense it signifies, Deliverance from evil. Now evil is distinguished into moral and natural. Moral evil is the evil of sin; and is called evil with relation to God, as it is the reverse of his nature, and the transgression of his law. Natural evil is the evil of suffering; and this is called evil with relation to us, on whom it is inflicted as a punishment for sin, and as it is painful to our nature.

Salvation, as it respects both moral and natural evil, implies a two-fold deliverance. First, a deliverance *out* of it: as when we see a man fallen into a river, we draw him *out*, and thereby save him from drowning.

In this sense we are saved when we are justified and sanctified, as we are then delivered *out* of that state of guilt, thraldom and misery in which we formerly lay. Secondly, a deliverance *from* it: as when we see a person on the brink of a river, and in danger of falling in, we lay hold on him, and prevent his falling, and thereby save him *from* the evil he was in danger of. In this sense, GOD saves us when he prevents our falling into some sin and misery which we are in danger of; and, in particular, when he prevents our falling into hell.

Again, the term Salvation is sometimes to be understood figuratively; and by a common figure, where the cause is put for the effect, signifies, The cause or means of salvation. And this is the primary and direct meaning of the term, salvation, in the text. This is evident from the preceding and subsequent words. In the first verse of this chapter the apostle says, " We ought to give the more earnest heed to the things which we have *heard*"—Observe, they are the things which we have HEARD with

our

our ears, that we are to take heed to. He then adds, verse 2. "For if the *word spoken* by angels was stedfast, and every transgression and disobedience—of that word, received a just recompence of reward," verse 3. "How shall we escape if we neglect so great salvation," or so great a WORD? "which at the first began to be SPOKEN by the Lord himself," &c. It is therefore certain, that by salvation the apostle here primarily intends the *word*, which was SPOKEN by our Lord; which was HEARD by his disciples, and which is greater than the word which was delivered by angels on mount Sinai.

But though he primarily intends the means of salvation, it is plain he does not intend them as separate from their end; from that actual salvation or deliverance from natural and moral evil before mentioned. This is evident from the whole epistle in general, and from many passages thereof in particular. In chap. iii. ver. 6. there is a caution against neglecting the confidence and the rejoicing of the hope: all which belong to the most spiritual nature

ture of our salvation. Ver. 12. we have a caution against an evil heart of unbelief. Ver. 13. one against being hardened through the deceitfulness of sin. Chap. iv. ver. 1. there is one against neglecting to enter into rest; that is, eternal life. In chap. x. ver. 38. there is one against neglecting to live by faith. Chap. xii. ver. 1. one against neglecting to lay aside every weight, and the sin which does so easily beset us. Ver. 14. we are not to neglect to follow peace and holiness. And, ver. 28. we are not to neglect to have, or hold fast *grace*. From all that has been said it is evident, that by salvation the apostle intended, first, the gospel in general, as the means of salvation, and, secondly, that actual salvation or deliverance from evil, which is obtained thereby.

And this the apostle calls, so great salvation. It is clear from the context, that, by a comparison of the law with the gospel, he intends to shew the superiority of the latter. And this he does by shewing that it was given, and promulged by a person who is vastly superior to those who

were

were employed in delivering all preceding dispensations. So chap. i. ver. 1. God at sundry times, and in divers manners, spake of old unto our fathers by the prophets; but now, in delivering the gospel, he has made use of his Son, whom he hath appointed the heir of all things, and by whom he made the world; who is the brightness of his Father's glory, and the express image of his person, and who upholds all things by the word of his power. This salvation, then, is as much superior to those former dispensations, as the almighty, and all-glorious Son of God is to weak and fallible men.

Again, chap. ii. ver. 2. The law was given by angels; but this salvation was given by the Lord himself. It is so glorious in its nature, and of such importance to the world, that no creature, or number of creatures, was capable of such a charge; therefore the Lord himself undertook the vast design. And on this account the gospel salvation is as eminently superior to the law, as the Creator and Lord of all is to a small part of his creatures.

II. Having

II. Having shewn what we are to understand by so great salvation, I proceed, Secondly, to enquire what is here meant by neglecting it; And that this important question may be fully answered, I shall first shew who the persons are whom the apostle supposes to be in danger of this neglect. And I shall be the more particular in doing this, because it is here that so many go astray in expounding these words: they mistake the persons intended by the apostle; and then they easily mistake the meaning of what is said unto them.

The persons intended by the apostle are frequently supposed to be such as are unbelieving, and unconverted. That these, in some sense, neglect this salvation is certain. Nevertheless, they are not the persons intended in the text. This is evident from hence; the persons intended by the apostle must be those to whom the epistle was written, and not those to whom it was not written. Now the epistle was not written, in whole or in part, to unbelivers, either Jews or Gentiles; of consequence, the apostle could not intend these when he said,

" How

"How shall we escape, if we neglect so great salvation?" But who then did he intend? Those Hebrews who had *heard* and *believed* the gospel, and who were *truly converted*, and made the *children of* God thereby. Therefore, said he, verse 1. "We ought to give the more earnest heed to the things which we have heard, lest at any time we should let them slip." We? who? WE CHRISTIAN BELIEVERS: WE CONVERTED HEBREWS. As if he had said, *I*, Paul, an apostle, who am a converted Hebrew myself, and who am the author of this epistle: and *you* to whom I send it, who are converted Hebrews also, ought to take the more earnest heed to the things—the truths of the gospel, which we—*you* and *I* have heard, lest at any time we, you and I, should let them slip. "For if the word spoken by angels was stedfast, and every transgression and disobedience received a just recompence of reward, How shall we"—CHRISTIAN BELIEVERS, "escape, if we neglect so great salvation?"

And that these Hebrews, were not mere professors, but rather genuine converts,

and

and real children of God, is evident from what is said of them, and attributed to them all over this epistle. So chap. iii. verse 1. they are called, " Holy brethren," and are said to be " partakers of the heavenly calling." And, first, they are called " brethren;" that is, children of the same Father, and members of the same family with the apostle. Secondly, they are called, " holy brethren;" that is, they were first made holy, and then set apart for holy purposes. Thirdly they are said to be partakers of the heavenly calling; that is, partakers of the gospel, and its spiritual benefits. So the Calvinian Assembly, in their annotation on the place, say, " Holy bre-
" thren."—" Such as were made holy by
" Jesus Christ."—" And he calls them
" brethren, not by merit, in respect of their
" carnal generation: but because they were
" ALL partakers of the same holy, and
" precious faith now with him:" and on these words, " Partakers of the heavenly calling. That is," say they, " EFFEC-
" TUAL CALLING†." So Mr. *Henry*,

the

† See the Assembly's Annotations.

the great oracle of our Calvinists, expounds the words: " Observe," says he, " 1. The " honourable appellation used to those to " whom he wrote.—Holy brethren, par- " takers of the heavenly calling. 1. Bre- " thren; not only, *my* brethren, but the " brethren of Christ, and in him brethren " to all the saints."—" 2. Holy brethren, " holy, not only in profession and title, but " in principle and practice, in heart and " life."—" 3. Partakers of the heavenly " calling, partakers of the means of grace, " and of the Spirit of grace that came down " from heaven, and by which christians " are EFFECTUALLY called out of darkness " into marvellous light||."

So the Calvinian *Wilson,* author of the Christian Dictionary, saith, " Holy Bre- " thren."—" Such as being sanctified by " the Spirit, are received into his fellow- " ship to be one with him*." To these testimonies I will add that of Dr. *Gill :* " Wherefore holy brethren."——" The " apostle calls the Hebrews BRETHREN, " not because they were of the same
" natu-

|| Hen. on the place. * Christ. Dict. on the place.

"natural stock and lineage, but because they were in the same SPIRITUAL relation: THEY ALL had the same father, belonged to the same family, were the adopted sons of God, the brethren of Christ, of one another, and of the apostle; and they were HOLY, not by birth, nor by external separation from other nations; but thro' sanctification of the Spirit.—Partakers of the heavenly calling. By which is meant—an internal, special call of grace, to the enjoyment of the blessings of grace here, and to glory hereafter‡."

If this, then, is not characteristic of a true Christian, it will be in vain to look for any thing that is, in all the book of God.

Verse 6. They are said to be the house of Christ; that is, his spiritual habitation, or place of abode. Again, they had confidence, and the rejoicing of the hope. And, first, they had hope; that is a well-grounded hope, or expectation of eternal life. Secondly, they had the rejoicing of the hope, the rejoicing which naturally belongs

‡ See Gill on the place.

belongs to, and is inseparably connected with it. And thirdly, they had confidence, παρρησιαν, a liberty of free profession of Chiist, in times of trouble: in other words, They had such hope of eternal life, through Christ, as caused them inwardly to rejoice in him, and to confess him outwardly with great boldness. Here, then, we have another proof, that the people supposed to be in danger of neglecting this great salvation, were the genuine children of God.

Verse 12. The apostle calls them "brethren," and the admonition given them supposes they had union with God.

Verse 14. They are said to be partakers of Christ. "*In hæreditate illâ cœlesti*," says *Piscator*, in that cœlestial inheritance, of which none are partakeis, but TRUE BELIEVERS[†]. The calvinian *Pool* tells us that *Syrus, Estius, Ribera*, and others comment thus on the place: "*Commixti sumus cum Christo, i. e. in unum corpus cum ipso coagmentati, ei per fidem insiti et incorporati, facti membra ejus, tandem et gloriæ:*" that is, we are mixed

---

[†] Piscator in loc.

ed together with Chrift: we are cemented
into one body with him: we are made his
members, partakers of his fpirit and grace,
and finally of his glory*. Mr. *Henry* fays,
" Here obferve, 1. The Saints privilege,
" They are made partakers of Chrift, that
" is, of the fpirit, nature, grace, righteouf-
" nefs, and life of Chrift; they are intereft-
" ed in all that is Chrift's, in all that he is,
" in all that he has done, or can do‖."

Again, they are faid to have " the beginning of confidence." The original
word, υποτασις, according to *Suicerus*, fignifies, confidence, reliance, or a foundation on which any one leans. So on chap.
xi. ver. 17. he fays, it means the fame
thing derived from the verb υριταμαι, which
fignifies, to bear up, not to yield; but to
ftand refolutely againft an adverfary†.
Oecumenius fays here, Αρχην της υποτασεως
την προς τον χριτον πιτιν φησι· δι αυτης γαρ υπετη-
μεν, Και γεγενημεθα μετοχοι τε χριτε, Faith in
Chrift is the beginning of our fubfiftence;
for by it we fubfift, and are made partak-

B 3

---

* Pool's Synop. Crit. in loc. ‖ Hen. on the place.
† Thef. Eccl.

ers of Christ*. So *Theodoret*, την πιςιν αρχην υποςασεως κεκληκε· δι εκεινης γαρ ενεκργυνθημεν, και συνηφθημεν τω δεσποτη χριςω, και της τε παναγιε πνευματος μετειληφωμεν χαριτος. He calls faith the beginning of our υποςασις; for by it we are renewed, and joined to the Lord Christ, and receive the grace of his most holy Spirit||. So *Theophylect*, την αρχην της υποςασεως, τουτεςι την πιςιν· δι αυτης γαρ υπεςημεν και εσιωθημεν την θειαν και πνευματικην εσιωσιν και αναγεννησιν· The beginning of our upostasis; that is faith; for by it we subsist, and receive the divine and spiritual essence and regeneration§. *Diodati*, the famous calvinian commentator, calls it, "The gift of God's Spirit and faith, "which is as the root by which we "live and subsist spiritually in Christ‡." And Dr. *Whitby* renders την αρχην υποςασεως, "The beginning of their hope. That "hope to which we have fled for refuge, "chap. vi. 18. That hope which causeth "us to rejoice. v. 6†.

Chap.

---

* Œcumenius in loc. || Theodoret in loc.
§ Theophylect in loc.   ‡ See Diodati on the place.
† See Whitby on the place.

Chap. 4. verse 3. They are said to have believed with the apostle, yea, and after the same manner; that is, they are said so to believe in Christ, as to enter into rest : into the rest of gospel grace, which implies peace of conscience, and power over sin ; and, also, that they had a right to, and a hope of the rest of eternal life.

Chap. 6. verse 4, 5. Here it is said that They were once enlightened, and had tasted of the heavenly gift, and were made partakers of the Holy Ghost, and had tasted of the good word of God, and the powers of the world to come. And here observe, 1. They *were once enlightened* —φωτισθεντας, enlightened with the true, spiritual knowledge of GOD. But it may be said, " The " antient fathers understood this of baptism, " which they called φωτισμος, illumination." True; but then they called it so on this supposition, that all who were baptized with water, were, at the same time, baptized with the Holy Ghost, and inwardly enlightened thereby. *Justin Martyr* says, " φωτισθεν-
" τας, (enlightened) signifies, those who
" having been instructed in the knowledge
" of

"of Christ, and then baptized, were far-
"ther enlightened by the divine Spirit†."
So the calvinian *Leigh*, in his Critica
Sacra tells us: "The greek fathers *sometimes* call φωτισμον, *baptismum*, and φωτιζω, *baptizo*: For those which are BAPTIZED WITH THE HOLY GHOST, THEIR MINDS ARE ILLUSTRATED WITH THE BEAMS OF DIVINE LIGHT." And when the apostle said, ye were ONCE enlightened, he meant, ye were TRULY and REALLY enlightened. So *Pool* on the place, " Semel hic idem
" quod *planè* et *verè*, απαξ pro απαξαπλως,
prorsus, perfectè, ut Heb. ix. 26, 28. That is, ONCE is one and the same with TRULY, REALLY, απαξ for απαξαπλως, ALTOGETHER, PERFECTLY, as Heb. ix. 26. 28. And he quotes *Ribera, Erasmus, Camero*, and several other divines of great note, who consider the persons here said to be enlightened as men who, " *absolutionem a præteri-*
" *tis omnibus peccatis suis acceperunt, &c.*
" *omnibusque christianorum privilegiis do-*
" *nati erant:*" that is, as men who have received the forgiveness of all their former
sins

† Apol. 1 Edit. Grabe. Sect. 80.

sins, and have all the privileges of Christians bestowed upon them*.

2. They had tasted of the heavenly gift; that is, the gift of grace in general, which came down from heaven. If any thing more particular is here intended, perhaps it is that which is elsewhere called, The gift of righteousness; that is, justification, or the remission of sins. Accordingly *Paræus* mentions *Erasmus*, and several other eminent divines, who say, the heavenly gift is, " *Fidem, quæ cœlitus datur illuminatis;*" faith which is given from above to those who are enlightened‡. And to taste of this does not mean a slight or superficial participation thereof; but rather a full and perfect one. In this sense we *must* understand the same word, as it is used, chap. ii. verse 9. where it is said that Christ *tasted* death for every man: certainly he partook of it in the most full and ample manner.

3. They were made partakers of the Holy Ghost; that is, they partook of the witness and fruit thereof. *Pool* tells us that *Grotius* understands it, " *Donorum et charis-*

---

* Syn. Crit. in loc.   ‡ Ibid.

" *charismatum Spiritus sancti, &c. quæ non*
" *contingebant eo tempore nisi justificatis,*"
of the gifts and graces of the Holy Spirit,
&c. which at that time were given to none
but the justified [*].

4. They had tasted as truly and fully as
Christ tasted death, the good word of God;
that is, they had experienced the nourishment and sweetness thereof, as truly as
Christ experienced the bitterness of death.
So *Grotius*, " *Gustare, hic et infra est experiendo cognoscere* :" that is, to taste here,
and in the next clause, means to KNOW
BY EXPERIENCE.

5. They had, in the same manner, tasted
the powers of the world to come; that is,
they had not only been partakers of the
gospel and its present benefits, which some
understand, by the world to come (rendering μελλοντος αιωνος, the future age; that is
the gospel age, to which the Mosaic was
prior;) but also of the powers, the enlivening and strengthening joys of eternity;
in other words, they had a foretaste of the
joys of heaven.

Estius,

---

[*] Ibid.

Estius, *Menochius* and *Ribera*, according to *Pool*, say, that the powers of the world to come mean, " *Immortalitatem et gloriam,* " *vitamque beatam, et eternam Dei visionem* " *in cœlis electis promissam in regno Christi:*" that is, immortality, glory, the beatific life, and eternal vision promised in heaven to the elect in the kingdom of Christ. And they add, that the Hebrews, " *dicuntur gus-* " *tasse, quia eas fide, amore, vel magno* " *desiderio perceperunt, earumque spe de-* " *lectabantur*"—are said to have tasted those powers, because they had a perception of them by faith, love, and a great desire, and were delighted by the hope of them: [the things they had tasted.]

Thus, by considering these five particulars *separately*, we find each of them so expressive of the spiritual nature, or properties of our holy religion, that it is absurd to affirm either of them of any but true believers. But if we consider them in connexion with each other, and as so many links of one chain, and suppose them *all* to be found in any but a real believer, the absurdity is much greater. But if we consider fider them altogether, and in connexion with their context, the abfurdity is greater ſtill by many degrees; feeing that, by fuch an interpretation, the coherence is entirely deſtroyed, and the whole paſſage turned into abfolute nonſenſe.

To make this appear, let it be obſerved, that in the two firſt verſes of this chapter, there is an exhortation for the Hebrew converts to go on unto perfection. That, verſe 3. the apoſtle adds, "And this will we do, if GOD permit:" that is, we will go on unto perfection. Then, verſe 4. that (as the calvinian *Diodati* tells us) the apoſtle "gives a reafon of the exhortation "of verſe 1." Well, then, let us fee what fort of a reafon it is, according to the calvinian interpretation. True believers are to go on unto perfection; *becauſe* it is impoſſible to renew hypocrites and falſe profeſſors again unto repentance, if they fall away from common, unſaving grace! Wonderful reafon indeed! and well worthy of the cauſe it is brought to fupport.—Let us next fee what fort of reafon it is, on fuppofition that the perfons mentioned in the

1ſt,

1st, 2d, and 3d verses, are the same with those mentioned in the 4th and 5th. Let us, Christian believers, go on unto perfection; because, if we do not, we shall do the reverse: that is, we shall forfeit and lose the grace we have. And when once this is lost we shall find it *morally* impossible, that is, very difficult, to recover it again. Now, according to this interpretation, the coherence is clear, and the argument strictly conclusive. It is therefore certain, that the persons mentioned in the passage under consideration, were not false professors, or hypocrites; but real children of GOD.

Again, verse 10. They had works and labour of love. 1. They had love, the love of GOD and of their neighbour. 2. They had works, good works proceeding from that love. 3. There was found in them labour of love: so great was their love, that it caused them not only to do such works as were good in their own nature; but also to labour in them, or do them with all their might. Agreeable to this, Mr. Henry faith, "God had wrought "a principle of holy love and charity in "them, which had discovered itself in "suitable works which would not be for- "gotten of God‖.

Verse 18. They *had* fled for refuge to lay hold on the hope set before them: which hope THEY HAD as an anchor of the soul, both SURE and STEADFAST. On this passage the learned *Suicerus* says, "*Metapho- "ricè vocatur spes Christiana, anchora animæ, "quæ in ipsa cælorum adyta penetrans, animam "nostram tutam ac firmam præstat adversus "omnes tentationum procellas:*" that is, The CHRISTIAN HOPE is metaphorically stiled, The anchor of the soul, which penetrating into the recesses of heaven, preserves the soul safe and steadfast against all the storms of temptation‡. So St. Chrysostom, Ωσπερ η αγκυρα εξαρτηθεισα τε πλοιε ουκ αφιησιν αυτο περιφερεσθαι, καν μυριοι παρασαλευσωσιν ανεμοι, αλλ εξαρτηθεισα εδραιον ποιει· ουτω και η ελπις; as the anchor cast into the sea, does not suffer the ship to be carried away by the waves, though

‖ Hen. on the place.   ‡ Suicerus page 63. a.

though the winds be contrary, but being thrown out renders her stedfast, so it is with Hope‡. Again he saith, Ορας της πιςεως το κατορθωμα, οτι ως αγκυρα τις ασφαλης, ετως εκβαλλει τον σαλον· οπερ εν και αυτος ο Παυλος τοις Εβραιοις επιςελλει, ετωσι λεγων περι της πιςεως· Ην ως αγκυραν εχομεν της ψυχης ασφαλη και βεβαιαν, και εισερχομενην εις το εσωτερον τε καταπετασματος. Ινα γαρ ακεσας αγκυραν, μη νομισης κατω καθελκεσθαι, δεικνυσιν, οτι καινη τις αυτη της αγκυρας η φυσις, ε κατω πιεζεσα, αλλ ανω κουφιζεσα την διανοιαν, και προς τον ερανον μεθιςωσα, και εις το εσωτερον τε καταπετασματος χειραγωγεσα· καταπετασμα γαρ ενταυθα τον ερανον εκαλεσε. That is, you see the excellency of faith, it will free you from every fluctuation; which *Paul* writes to the Hebrews, speaking thus of it; which we have as an anchor of the soul, sure and stedfast, and enters in within the veil. For, lest you should think, when you hear speak of an anchor, that it will pull you downward, he shews you that it is an anchor of a new kind, which does not depress the mind, but raises it up to Heaven, and leads you as by the hand to those things which

‡ Chrysost. Hom. II.

are within the veil; for in this place he calls Heaven, the veil*. Hence Mr. *Henry,* speaking of this hope, saith, " 1. It is *sure* " in its own nature, for it is the special " work of GOD in the soul, it is a good " hope through grace; it is not a flattering " hope made out of a spider's web, but " it is a true work of GOD, it is a strong " and substantial thing. 2. It is *steadfast* as " to its object; it is an anchor that has " taken good hold, it enters into that which " is within the veil, it is an anchor that is " cast upon the rock, the Rock of ages; " it does not think to fasten in the sands, " but enters within the veil, and fixes there " upon Christ; he is the object, he is the " anchor-hold of the believer's hope ‡."

Chap. x. 23. They had the same kind of faith with the apostle, and had made the same profession of it. Verse 26. They had received the knowledge of the truth. Verse 29. They were sanctified by the blood of the covenant. Verse 32. They had been illuminated, and had endured a great fight of

---

* Ibid.   ‡ Hen. on the place.

of affliction: or as Mr. Henry faith, "They had suffered, in former days after they were illuminated; that is, as soon as God had breathed life into their souls, and caused divine light to spring up in their minds, and taken them into favour and covenant*."

Verse 34. They had taken joyfully the spoiling of their goods, KNOWING IN THEMSELVES THAT THEY HAD IN HEAVEN A BETTER AND AN ENDURING SUBSTANCE.

Verse 35. THEY HAD A CONFIDENCE WHICH HAD A GREAT RECOMPENCE OF REWARD: which, according to Mr. Henry, "carries a present reward in it, in holy peace, and joy, and much of God's presence and power resting upon them; and it shall have a great recompence of reward hereafter‖."

Verse 39. At the very time the apostle wrote to them, They *believed* TO THE SAVING OF THEIR SOULS.

Chap. xii. 22—24. They were come to Mount Zion, and unto the city of the living God,

---

* Hen. on the place. ‖ Ibid.

God, the heavenly Jerusalem, and to the innumerable company of angels; to the general assembly of the church of the first-born which are written in heaven, to God the Judge of all, and to the spirits of just men made perfect, and to Jesus the Mediator of the new covenant, and to the blood of sprinkling which speaketh better things than the blood of Abel. The eight particulars mentioned in this passage are a compendium of the privileges of the christian church; and when the apostle said that these Hebrews were come unto these, his meaning was, that they truly and spiritually enjoyed them. Accordingly Mr. Henry saith, "In coming to Mount Zion, believers "come into heavenly places, and into a "heavenly society. 1. Into heavenly "places; the city of the living God"— "There his people may find him ruling, "guiding, sanctifying and comforting "them; there he speaks to them by the "gospel ministry; there they speak to him "by prayer, and he hears them; there he "trains them up for heaven, and gives "them the earnest of their inheritance."—

2. To

" 2. To a heavenly Society. 1. To an in-
" numerable company of angels, who are
" of the same family with the saints."—
" 2. To the general assembly, and church
" of the first-born that are written in hea-
" ven, that is, to the universal church,
" however dispersed. By faith we come to
" them; have communion with them in
" the same head, by the same spirit, and in
" the same blessed hope, and walk in the
" same way of holiness*."

Add to all that hath been said, as a farther proof that these Hebrews were genuine Christians, that the apostle hath numbered them with himself, as members of the same family, and as partakers of the same christian privileges, not less than FIFTY times, as may be seen in the following places. Chap. i. 2. chap. ii. 1, 2, 3, 8, 9. chap. iii. 1. 6. 14, 15, 16. chap. iv. 1, 2, 3. 11. 14, 15, 16. chap. v. 11. chap. vi. 1. 3. 18, 19, 20. chap. vii. 26. chap. viii. 1. chap. ix. 12. 24. chap. x. 10. 15. 20. 22. 24, 25, 26. 30. 39. chap. xi. 3. 40.

* See Henry on the place.

3 40. chap. xii. 1, 2..9, 10. 25. 28, 29. chap. xiii. 10. 13. 14, 15.

It is therefore certain, upon the whole, that these Hebrews, who are supposed to be in danger of neglecting this salvation, were true believers, were real christians, and genuine children of GOD.

I now proceed in the next place to shew, what the apostle meant by their neglecting this great Salvation.

And, first, it certainly does not mean, that they had neglected to embrace it. This is evident from what hath already been said, concerning their being true believers, and real children of God : for it is certain that if they had neglected to embrace or receive this salvation, they could not be true, genuine christians, they could not be the real children of GOD : seeing it was only by embracing, or receiving this salvation that they partook of this privilege, and were brought into this number.

And that they did not neglect to embrace this salvation, is particularly evident, 1. From those places which assert that they *had formerly* SOUGHT *and* OBTAINED it : as
chap.

chap. vi. 18. where it is said that they *had fled for refuge, to lay hold on the hope set before them.* 2. From those places where it is said that they were, *at that time*, IN POSSESION *of it*. as chap. vi. ver. 19. where the apostle saith, *which hope* WE HAVE &c. chap. xii. ver. 22—24, where he tells them, We ARE come to Mount Zion, &c. and chap. iii. ver. 1. where he tells them that they are PARTAKERS of the heavenly calling. It is therefore undeniably evident, that these Hebrews had not neglected to seek and embrace this salvation; and, of consequence, that whatever the apostle intended by neglecting it, he could not possibly intend this.

But what then did he intend? Neglecting to PERSEVERE therein: or, which comes to the same, by neglecting this salvation he meant, APOSTASY, TOTAL and FINAL apostasy from it.

By *apostasy* I mean, simply falling away from it. By *total* apostasy I mean, falling away, 1. From the spirit of it. 2. From the practice of it. and 3. From the profession of it. By *final* apostasy, I mean, to fall

fall away thus, and rife no more forever.

Now, that this apoftafy was the evil which the apoftle fuppofed thefe Hebrews to be in danger of, and which, in this epiftle, he has been labouring to prevent; and, of confequence, is what he intended by neglecting this great falvation, I hope to demonftrate very largely from all parts of the epiftle. And the method I intend to purfue is, Firft, to point out fuch particular paffages, as prove the whole propofition, or any part of it; and then, Secondly, by way of confirmation of the truth held forth in thefe paffages, to add a general furvey of the *occafion* and *defign* of the whole epiftle, and the manner of the apoftle's reafoning therein.

And, Firft, I am to point out fuch particular paffages as prove the whole propofition or any part of it.

And, 1. We will confider chap. ii. ver. 1. " We ought to give the more earneft heed to the things which we have heard, left at any time we fhould let them flip," μηποτε παραρρυωμεν. Dr. *Hammond* tells us that " Παραρρυωμεν, is a phrafe ufed from the
" water,

"water, which when it is not kept within
"limits, falls away and, runs out‡."

Dr. *Owen*, the great champion of the Calvinists in the last century, observes on the place, that "παραρρυωμεν, is no where "else used in the New Testament;" and that as it stands connected with μηποτε, it means, "Lest we fall; fall down; that is, perish*." So is the word interpreted by St. Chrysostom, μηποτε παραρρυωμεν, τστεστι μη απολωμεθα, μη εκπεσωμεν, *that we* PERISH NOT; *that we* FALL NOT§. *Pool*, on the authority of *Camero*, *Erasmus*, *Estius*, *Gerhardus* and *Beza*, says, "Hæc locutio, &c. "*est metaphora ducta ab aqua, quæ nisi quo-* "*dam conceptaculo contineatur, facile defluit;* "*quæ inutiliter effluit; quæ prorsus et irre-* "*parabiter perit:*" that is, This expression is a metaphor taken from water, which, if it is not contained in some proper vessel, easily runs off, flows away to no purpose, and is entirely and irreparably lost‖. And *Grotius*, speaking of this very

passage

‡ See Hammond on the place.   * See Dr. Owen on the Epistle to the Heb.   § Chrysostom in loc.
‖ Synop. Crit. in loc.

passage saith, "*Nihil hic cavere jubemur, quod non et fieri possit, et sæpè fiat:*" that is, the apostle bids us here beware of nothing, but what MAY, and DOES *frequently* happen§. The calvinian author of Critica Sacra renders it, "let slip, like water put "into a cullender or riven dish‖." Our margin renders it, Run out as leaking vessels. From which I would observe, 1. That the converted Hebrews had the water of this salvation in the vessels of their mind or heart. 2. That these vessels were leaky, that is, liable to let it slip or run out. 3. That if the Hebrews did not take earnest heed, this would certainly be the case: this salvation would slip, or run out of their hearts; that is, they would lose it by apostasy.

The learned Dr. *Whitby* renders μηποτε παραρρυωμεν, "lest we fall off from them;" that is, from the things which we have "heard:" and he quotes *Oecumenius, Theophylact* and *Phavorinus*, as agreeing with him*. *Diodati* expounds it, "Let them "slip

§ See Grotius in k c.
‖ See Critica Sacra, page 430. * Whitby on the place.

" flip, that is to fay, that we may not go
" away from the Communion of Christ and
" his church, nor forsake his faith and
" service.*" Mr. *Baxter's* comment is,
" Lest by negligence or unbelief, we
" should lose what we have heard, and be
" as leaking vessels, and be lost ourselves‡."
Mr. *S. Clark* renders it, " Run out as leak-
" ing vessels"—" viz. out of our heads,
" hearts, or practice, so as to depart from
" THE FAITH or service of Christ†." The
Assembly of Divines, on this passage tell
us, that " From the former doctrine touch-
" ing Christ's excellency"—" St. Paul in-
" fers this following exhortation. The
" scope whereof," they say, " is, to stir up
" the Hebrews to STAND FAST in that
" FAITH which THEY HAD RECEIVED§."
The Continuators of *Pool* tell us, that
" All forgetfulness of memory, all APOS-
" TASY IN HEART or profession is that
" which the Spirit forbiddeth in this meta-
" phor, παραρρυωμεν‖." Mr. *Christopher Love* ex-

---

* See Critica Sacra, page 430. ‡ Baxter on the place. † Clark on the place. § Assembly's Annot. on the place. ‖ Pool's Comment on the place.

expounds it, "Left we let them flip, as a "broken and leaking veffel runs out; for "μηποτε παραρρυωμεν, is a metaphor taken "from leaking veffels*." Dr. *Gill* obferves, that " The vulgate Latin verfion "renders it, Left we fhould run out; and "the Syriac verfion, Left we fhould fall; "and the Arabic verfion, Left we fhould "fall from honefty‡." Father *Quefnel* faith, " We muft not be like leaking "veffels out of which the water runs†." The Dutch Annotators, as ordered by the Synod of Dort, fay, " This is by fome "underftood of the word which we have "heard, and we muft take care that the "fame in us does not run out, or leak "through, as is wont to come to pafs in "forgetful hearers. By others it is under"ftood of perfons themfelves, who are faid "to run out, when like water that runs "out, they perifh, or are loft§." Mr. *Deering*, B. D. faith, " The apoftle ufeth "a metaphor taken from old tubs, which
"run

---

* Combat between the Flefh and the Spirit, page 191. ‡ Gill on the place. † Quefnel on the New Teftament. § See Dutch Annotat. as publifhed by Authority in 1637.

"run out at the joints, and can hold no "liquor"—"So we, if we take into us "the sweet wine of the word of Christ, as "into"—"broken vessels that it run out "again, we become altogether unprofita"ble, all goodness falleth away, and we "become as water poured on the ground— "and is never after profitable any more*." Once more: The author of Critica Sacra, in his Annotations, and the learned *John Trapp*, in his Commentary (both Calvinists), tell us that "the *Arabic* renders it, "lest we FALL," and the *Syriac*, "lest "we PERISH"—"Accordingly, saith Dr. Hammond, "*Theophylact* hath μη εκπεσωμεν, "μη απολωμεθα, Let us not FALL AWAY, "let us not PERISH‡."

From all that hath been said, it is evident that the apostle here supposes the Hebrews to be in danger of apostasy; and (if the *Syriac* Interpreters, *Theophylact, Chrysostom, Erasmus, Camero, Estius, Gerhardus, Beza, Pool, Owen, Hammond, Baxter, Deering*, and the Dutch Annotators may be

D 2   de-

---

* See Deering's Lectures, published in 1590.   ‡ Dr. Hammond on the place.

depended on) of such apostasy as would occasion the apostate to PERISH FOR EVER; and therefore it can be no other than total and final apostasy which is here intended.

2. We will consider Chap. III. verse 6. " But Christ as a Son over his own house, whose house are we, IF WE HOLD FAST the confidence and the rejoicing of the hope FIRM UNTO THE END." By the end the apostle certainly meant, the end of life. And when he said that we *are* the house of Christ, if we hold fast the confidence, &c. firm unto the end, it was impossible he should mean, that the goodness of their PRESENT STATE depended on their future conduct; because this would be to suppose the effect to precede the cause. Nor could he mean that their future conduct would be an evidence of their being the house of Christ at present. For in the first place, such an evidence would prove too much. For if what a man does to-morrow will prove that he is in a right state to-day, it will equally prove that he was so yesterday; and, if so, it will equally prove that

he was so the day before, and so on to the first day of his existence: from whence it will follow, that if he ever does right in future, he was always the house of Christ, or in a right state and condition. Secondly, such an evidence would be useless. It is certain no argument can prove any thing, before that argument exists. Now the circumstance of holding our confidence firm unto the end, will not exist before the end, or rather, till after it: at which time there will be no need of any such evidence of our being the house of Christ, at any particular time, while we were here on earth. All that will be necessary to be known of this matter, will then be declared more effectually a thousand other ways; and, therefore, this sort of evidence will be as useless then, as the light of a feeble taper would now be in the presence of the noon-day sun. Once more: that this interpretation is false, appears from hence, that it has nothing to do with the scope of the epistle. " This," as the learned and celebrated *John Goodwin* has told us, " was not to teach the He-
" brews to know whether they were true
" believers

"believers or no, at present, much less to teach them this knowledge by what they should approve themselves to be, at the day of their death, (which had been to give men darkness to see by!) but to animate, encourage, urge and press them to continue constant in the faith, which at present they had embraced, and made profession of, unto the end[*]." It is absurd, to suppose that the apostle would say, If we hold fast our confidence, &c. to the end, this will at, and after the end demonstrate that we are now, this day, the house of Christ!—But if this is not his meaning, what then does he mean? I answer: that as we are his present house or habitation, by a present participation of this confidence, &c. so we are intended for, yea, and actually shall be his eternal abode, on supposition that we hold fast these graces unto the end of our life. Hence St. *Cyprian* on the place, as quoted by *Erasmus*, saith, "*Nativitas salutaris non accepta, sed custodita vivificat:*" it is not

---

[*] See Redem. Redeemed, page 260.

a SAVING birth RECEIVED, but KEPT, that vivifies: (he means, that vivifies in eternity*.)

From what has been said, it follows, 1. That the apostle supposed it possible for the converted Hebrews not to hold the confidence, &c. firm unto the end. 2. That if they did not, they would not be the house of Christ always, though they were once so. Hence Dr. *Heylin* saith, " We are " that his house, if we stedfastly persevere " to the end in that confidence and hope " which we have so good reason to boast " of†." So *Estius*, and *Ribera:* " *Tacitè* " *eos hortatur ad perseverantiam in vocati-* " *one sua, in spe et fide, ne reverti velint ad* " *legem Mosis, ne inutile eis sit bene incepisse.*" He [the apostle] tacitly exhorts them to perseverance in their vocation, hope, and faith, lest they return to the law of Moses; lest their good beginning should come to nothing§. This therefore is another proof that total and final apostasy was the evil which the apostle, in this epistle was labouring

---

* Erasm. in loc. † Heylin on the place. § Poli Syn. in loc.

labouring to prevent; and, of consequence, what he intended by, NEGLECTING THIS GREAT SALVATION.

3. Another proof of the point we have, chap. iii. verse 12. "Take heed, brethren, left there be in any of you an evil heart of unbelief, in departing from the living GOD." The original word, Αποςασια, is rendered, *defection*, and signifies a defection, or falling away from that which we formerly stood to. *Ribera* and *Estius*, as quoted by the calvinian *Pool*, say, that an evil heart of unbelief, means here, an heart " *Abjecta* " *fide Christi ad judaismum rediens*," returning to judaism after throwing away the faith of Christ||. Mr. *Henry* says, that " An evil heart of unbelief is at the bot-" tom of all our sinful departures from " GOD; it is a leading step to *apostasy*; if " once we allow ourselves to distrust GOD, " we may soon desert him."—And his observation on this passage is, that " CHRIS-" TIAN BRETHREN *have need to be* CAU-" TIONED *against* APOSTASY*." Bishop *Hall* saith, " Take heed, brethren, left
" after

|| Pol. Syn. in loc. * Hen. on the place.

"after this holy profession, made by you, there be found in any of you an evil and unbelieving heart, to fall away, and depart from the colours of the living God, to take part with infidelity*." Mr. *Wilson*, author of the Christian Dictionary saith, "To depart from God, signifies to fall away from God by infidelity†." Mr. *Perkins* says, "The author to the Hebrews shews five degrees of apostasy, by which the illumination of the gospel is turned into darkness; Heb. iii. 12. saying, Take heed lest there be in any of you an evil heart of unbelief, &c. Where the first degree is, consenting unto sin, being deceived with the temptation to it. The second is, hardness of heart upon practices of sin. Thirdly, the heart being hardened becomes unbelieving, and calls the truth of God into question. Fourthly, by unbelief it becomes evil, having a base conceit of the gospel. Fifthly, this evil heart brings a man to apostasy and falling from God

---

* Bp. Hall on the place. † See Christian Dictionary on the Epistle to the Hebrews.

"God, which is the extinguishing of the "light of the Gospel†." The calvinian author of Critica Sacra says, it signifies, "A SPIRITUAL DEPARTURE FROM GOD, "Heb. iii. 12." This witness is true. For according to the apostle, it is the HEART which departs from GOD IN the act of unbelief. Now, as faith is the root of all inward holiness, and this the root of all outward obedience; so unbelief is the root of all inward unholiness, and this of all outward disobedience. Therefore, whenever the heart departs from faith to unbelief, the consequence will be, that it will depart from holiness to sin: and then, in consequence of this, there will be an outward departure from an holy, to an unholy conversation. Again, the very learned Mr. *John Gregory*, formerly chaplain of Christchurch, Oxford, tells us, "The Arabic "is,"—"An obdurate and unbelieving "heart; and which goeth far, or QUITE "away from the living GOD:" on which he observes, "This is that heart of un-
"belief

---

† See Third Vol. of Perkins's Works, page 174.

"belief which we are bid here to take heed
"of; this looseth ALL our hold, and UT-
"TERLY estrangeth us from the life of GOD,
"and leaveth us ALTOGETHER without him
"in the world*." The calvinian continuators of *Pool* say, that the departing from the
living GOD here spoken of implies, "Turn-
"ing away, standing off, and separating
"the heart; it implies in it a *real*, TOTAL,
"and FINAL defection; actual and formal
"apostasy from him whom THEY HAD
"OWNED and RECEIVED."—"So that to
"apostatize from him [Christ] and his
"religion, is to apostatize from GOD, and
"to renounce ETERNAL LIFE, and to
"subject *themselves* to ETERNAL PUNISH-
"ment‖." This passage, then, is another
proof, that the apostle was speaking,
not only of apostasy; but, also, of TOTAL
and FINAL apostasy.

4. Again, verse 13. "But exhort one
another daily, while it is called To-day,
lest any of you be hardened through the
deceitfulness of sin. *Estius*, as quoted by
Pool,

* Gregory on the place.
‖ See Pool's Comment on the place.

Pool, says, that here we must understand by sin, "*Hunc actum peccati, qui est deficere a Christo, ut precedentia et sequentia satis declarant* ||:" that act of sin, which consists in falling away from Christ, as what precedes and follows sufficiently declare. The original word, σκληρυνθη, which is here rendered *hardened*, is the same as that in Acts xix. 9. where the unbelieving Jews, who would not receive *Paul's* preaching, are said to be hardened. Now concerning their hardness, we may observe three things: 1. They were so hardened, that they would not be persuaded to *believe* St. Paul's preaching. 2. They were so hardened as to *blaspheme* it before the multitude. 3. They were so hardened as to cause the apostle to *give them up* to a reprobate mind. And, therefore, it seems that their disorder was incurable; that it was *total* and *final* hardness.

Again, the hardness which the apostle supposed these Hebrews to be in danger of, he compares to that which excluded the antient Hebrews from the land of Canaan. So

---

|| Synop. Crit. in loc.

So verse 8. "Harden not your hearts, as in the provocation, as in the day of temptation in the wilderness:" verse 9. "When your fathers tempted me, proved me, and saw my works forty years." verse 10. "Wherefore I was grieved with that generation, and said, They do always err in their hearts, and they have not known my ways." verse 11. "So I sware in my wrath, They shall not enter into my rest."

Now, concerning these Israelites I observe, 1. That they had seen much of the goodness of God. 2. That they had a promise of greater favours. 3. That, for awhile, they believed and obeyed God, according as he had required of them. But, 4. they did not continue to do this. By this means, 5. God was so grieved with them, that he sware in his wrath, They shall never enter into my rest. In consequence of this, 6. They never did enter in.

Now the parallel intended by the apostle is this: 1. As your fathers saw much of the goodness of God in Egypt, the Red sea, and the wilderness; so have you seen much

of it in what he has already done for your souls, in the gospel of his Son. 2. As they had a promise of a greater blessing, even the land of Canaan, that land of rest, flowing with milk and honey; so have you a promise of the heavenly Canaan, that land of eternal peace and plenty. 3. As they, for a while, believed and obeyed in such a manner as they ought; so, also, have you. 4. As they did not continue to believe and obey; so you are in danger of following their example in this particular. 5. As they, for want of continuing in well-doing, provoked GOD to swear in his wrath that they should never enter into his rest; in like manner you will provoke him to swear in his wrath that you shall never enter into heaven, if you apostatize as they did. 6. In consequence of this oath they never did enjoy the PROMISED land; even so, if you provoke him as they did, you shall never enter the kingdom of heaven. This then is another incontestable proof, that neglecting this salvation, unto TOTAL AND FINAL APOSTASY, was the evil which the apostle
appre-

apprehended these Hebrews to be in danger of.

5. Verse 14. "We are partakers of Christ, saith the apostle, καταχωμεν, if we hold fast the beginning of our confidence steadfast unto the end." *Baxter's* comment is, " We are initially made partak-
" ers of Christ as our Saviour: but if we
" will attain salvation by him, we must
" hold the subsisting faith (or the confi-
" dence) in which we have begun—firm
" unto the end: (for perseverance is made
" a condition of the promise of salvation)||."
Grotius on the words says, " *Jus nati su-*
" *mus ut participemus de Christi claritate;*
" *sed jus pendens, datum sub conditione per-*
" *severandi.*" That is, We have got the right to partake of Christ's glory; but that right given us is suspended upon the condition of persevering‡. *Calvin* says, " Lau-
" *dat, quod bene cæperint. Sed ne prætextu*
" *gratiæ, quam consequuti sunt, carnis in-*
" *dulgeant securitati, dicit opus esse perseve-*
" *rantiâ. Nam plerique delibato tantum*

evan-

|| Baxter on the place. ‡ Grotius in loc.

" *evangelio, quasi ad summum pervenerint,*
" *de profectu non cogitant. Ita fit, ut non*
" *modo in medio studio, adeoque propè ipsos*
" *carceres desideant, sed alio vertunt cursum*
" *suum. Speciosa quidem est ista objectio,*
" *quid ultrà volumus, postquam adepti sumus*
" *Christum? Verum si fide possidetur, in eâ*
" *perstandum est, ut nobis perpetua maneat*
" *possessio. Ergo hac lege se nobis fruendum*
" *dedit Christus, ut eâdem quâ in ejus partici-*
" *pationem admissi sumus fide, tantum bonum*
" *conservemus usque ad mortem:*" That is, He [St. Paul] commends them that they had begun well. But left under a pretence of that grace, which THEY HAD OBTAINED, they should indulge a carnal security, he tells them they had need of perseverance. For many, having only tasted lightly of the gospel, do not so much as think of any proficiency, as if they were come to the highest already. Thus it cometh to pass, that they do not only sit down in the midst of the race, yea sometimes at the very entrance of the race; but TURN THEIR COURSE QUITE ANOTHER WAY. This indeed is a very specious objection,

When

When we have gotten Christ, what should we desire more? But if Christ be possessed by faith, we must persist in faith, that our possession in this kind may be perpetual. Therefore Christ hath given himself to be enjoyed by us, upon these terms, or by this law, that as we are admitted by faith to a PARTICIPATION OF HIM, so we should BY THE SAME FAITH PERSEVERE, and keep so great a good until death*. Dr. *Heylyn* saith, "We are made partakers "of Christ upon condition that we retain, "inviolably to the end, that hope in him "which we had at the beginning‡." Mr. *Sam. Clark*'s comment is, "Take heed of "apostasy, and be careful to persevere; "because all your interest in Christ de- "pends hereupon§." Mr. *Flavel* expounds the words thus: "If we have "followed him through many sufferings "and troubles, and shall turn away from "him at last, we lose all that we have "wrought and suffered in religion, and "shall never reach home to God at last:

"the

---

* Calvin in loc. ‡ Heylin on the place. § Clarke on the place.

"the crown of life belongs only to them who are faithful to the death*." Now, from this passage, and from what has been said on it by these great and learned divines, (both *Arminians* and *Calvinists*) I conclude, that apostasy is the evil which the apostle has here been labouring to prevent; and therefore, that it is this which he intended by, neglecting so great salvation.

6. A sixth proof of the point in hand we have, chap. iv. verse 11. "Let us labour, therefore, to enter into that rest, lest any man FALL after the same example of unbelief." From hence we learn, 1. That the evil which the apostle supposed the Hebrews to be in danger of, was, FALLING. 2. That it was, falling after the example of the Israelites of old.——Though it has been largely considered already, in what manner these fell, I shall again, briefly enquire into two things. The first is, How far they fell? and the second, By what means? As to the first, They fell TOTALLY and FINALLY from the PROMISE which
GOD

---

* Flavel's Works, Vol. I, p. 320. Second Edit.

God had given them: that is, they totally and finally fell short of possessing that rest, which God had promised they should possess. This is an undeniable and undoubted matter of fact. But, secondly, By what means did they thus fall? By unbelief or disobedience (for the original word, απειθεια, signifies either.) That this was the cause of their apostasy is evident from chap. iii. verse 17. where it is said that their carcases fell in the wilderness, because they had *sinned*; and from verse 19; where it is said, that they could not enter in because of unbelief: Compare this with chap. iv. verse 6. But let it be well remembered, that it was not because they had never believed and obeyed, that they could not enter in; but because they did not continue to do it.

Now on this I would observe, that it was impossible for the converted Hebrews to fall after this example, as the apostle saith, without, first, falling totally and finally, as they did. Nor, secondly, could they do it after this example, but by discontinuing to believe and obey. And

I

(54)

I would observe once more, that when the apostle exhorted these Hebrews to labour that they might not fall after this example, he certainly supposed that there was a possibility of their doing it. The truth of this is so evident, that the calvinian continuators of *Pool* have, by the force of evidence, been constrained to confess it. "The particle ʋ, (say they) may "be read *into*, and then it implies, lest any "of you prove rebels and apostates. Or "it is read *by*, or *after*, and then it is a "fall to DESTRUCTION AND HELL, with "all the miseries that those feel who are "shut out of GOD's rest‖." *Baxter's* comment on the place is, " Let it then be the " care and diligence of your heart and life, " to attain the rest, and not to lose it by " apostasy*." Dr. *Heylyn* saith, " Let us " therefore hasten diligently to enter into " that rest, lest any of us, imitating the disobedience of the Israelites, should perish as they did ‡. So the author of the Christian Dictionary. " To FALL—to *perish*,
or

‖ Pool's Comment on the place.   * Baxter in loc.
‡ Heylyn in loc.

or be *destroyed**." This therefore is another demonstration, that TOTAL and FINAL apostasy was the evil intended by neglecting this great salvation.

7. To the same purpose is verse 14. of the same chapter. "Seeing then that we have an high-priest that is passed into the heavens, Jesus the Son of God, let us HOLD FAST, ομολογιας, OUR PROFESSION, or *confession*. The not holding fast their profession, or apostatizing from it, is what the apostle apprehended the Hebrews to be here in danger of. And in supposing them to be in danger of apostatizing from their profession, he supposed them to be in danger of TOTAL apostasy; seeing their profession was that part of their religion which was easiest kept, and of consequence, that which they would retain the longest: they would, first, let go the life and spirit of their religion; then, secondly, the practice of it; and then, thirdly, and lastly, the profession of it. Hence Mr. *Henry*, on the place, saith,

---

* Christ. Dict. on the place.

faith, "Let us hold faſt the enlightening "doctrines of Chriſtianity in our heads, "and the ENLIVENING PRINCIPLES OF IT "IN OUR HEARTS, and the open profeſ- "ſion of it in our lips, and our practical "and univerſal ſubjection to it in our lives. "Obſerve here, 1. We ought to be poſ- "ſeſſed of the doctrines, principles, and "practice of the Chriſtian life. 2. *When* "*we are ſo,* WE MAY BE IN DANGER OF "LOSING OUR HOLD, from the corruption "of our hearts, the temptations of Satan, "and the allurements of this evil world. 3. "That the excellency of the High-Prieſt "of our profeſſion, would make our APOS- "TASY FROM HIM moſt heinous and inex- "cuſable; it would be the greateſt folly, "and the baſeſt ingratitude. 4. CHRIS- "TIANS muſt not only SET OUT WELL, "but *they muſt* HOLD OUT; *they that* EN- "DURE TO THE END *ſhall be ſaved, and* "NONE BUT THEY‖."

8. The next proof of the point we have, chap. vi. verſe 4—8. "For it is impoſſible
for

‖ Henry on the place.

for thofe who were once enlightened, and have tafted the heavenly gift, and were made partakers of the Holy Ghoft, and have tafted the good word of God, and the powers of the world to come; if they FALL AWAY, to renew them again unto repentance: feeing they crucify to themfelves the Son of God afrefh, and put him to an open fhame. For the earth which drinketh in the rain that cometh oft upon it, and bringeth forth herbs meet for them by whom it is dreffed, receiveth bleffing from God. But that which beareth thorns and briers, is rejected, and is nigh unto curfing, whofe end is to be burned."

That falling away is the evil intended in this paffage, is evident from verfe 6. where the apoftle fays, Και παραπεσοντας, If they FALL AWAY, &c. But it may be faid, "The apoftle fpeaks nothing pofitively "concerning falling away; he only fpeaks "on fuppofition, *if they fall away.*" To this I anfwer, 1. Suppofe we allow that the apoftle fpake only on fuppofition; it is certain that a fuppofition made by the Holy Ghoft in this manner, infers the conclufion
as

as fully as the strongest affirmation. For it would be great impiety to say, that the blessed and holy God makes use of vain, groundless, and impossible suppositions in dealing with his people. So the learned *Junius* saith on the place: " *Si non possit* " *fieri ut justus vel credens aliquis deficeret,* " *neque hypothesin hanc facturus esset aposto* " *lus, neque ex hypothesi tam grave pronun-* " *ciatum allaturus, neque ad hanc causam quæ* " *agitur, hoc dictum Hebræis, quibus scribe-* " *bat, accommodaturus.*" That is, If there were no possibility that a righteous man, or a believer might fall away, neither would the apostle have made this hypothesis or supposition, nor would he have inferred so grave or weighty a saying upon the supposition; nor would he have applied this saying to the Hebrews, to whom he wrote, in the cause which was now in hand‡. So the author of a book entitled " *Absolute Elec-* " *tion and Reprobation fully detected,*" saith on the place, " Now the graces which the " apostle here speaketh of, are not ordinary " or common; but special and excellent
" graces

‡ Junius in Parallel. ad Heb.

(59)

"graces; such as illumination, faith, a "relish of God's word, and a taste of hea- "ven. And the persons spoken of are "apostates, such as are under a possibility "of falling away for ever, and conse- "quently reprobates. whereas if it were "impossible that good men should fall "from grace, it would be absurd and ridi- "culous in the apostle to warn against it; "because no solid exhortation can be built "on a danger not possible to come to "pass||." But, 2. I deny that here is any supposition at all. For the word, *if*, is not in the original. Mr. *Wesley* has justly observed, that "The words are, Αδυνατον τυς απαξ φωτισθενίας—και παραπεσοντας. That "is, in plain English, it is impossible to "renew again unto repentance, those who "were once enlightened and have fallen "away‡." Dr. *Whitby* renders και παραπεσοντας, "and yet fall away*." It is therefore certain, as *John Goodwin* has well observed, that here is no "Hypothetical sign
F   "or

|| Ibid. See page 157, 158. ‡ Predestination calmly considered, page 65. Third Edit. * Discourse on the Five Points, page 404. 3d edit.

"or conditional particle [†]:" and therefore I conclude, that the apostle was not speaking of an imaginary falling away, which in reality, could never happen, but of such as was very possible in itself, and which the Christian Hebrews were in very great danger of. The venerable Archbishop *Cranmer* quotes this passage in proof of the possibility of the falling away of those who are justified: "It is NO DOUBT," said he, "but although WE BE ONCE JUSTIFIED, YET WE MAY FALL THEREFROM, by our own free will and consenting unto sin, and following the desires thereof. For albeit the house of our conscience be once made clean, and the foul spirit be expelled from us by baptism or penance, yet if we wax idle and take not heed, he will return with seven worse spirits, and possess us again. AND ALTHOUGH WE BE ILLUMINATED, AND HAVE TASTED THE HEAVENLY GIFT, AND BE MADE PARTAKERS OF THE HOLY GHOST: YET MAY WE FALL AND DISPLEASE GOD.
"Where-

[†] Redemption Redeemed, page 283, Sect. 18.

"Wherefore as St. *Paul* saith, He that "standeth, let him take heed that he fall "not*." Dr. *Heylyn* saith, If they fall away, means, " If they apostatize‡." The Dutch Annotators on the place say, " And "falling away [or falling,] whereby "we are not to understand all kinds of sins "whereinto true believers sometimes fall, "as David, Peter, &c. who afterwards "came to repentance; but a total fall-"ing, or apostasy from the Christian "religion§."

But what kind of falling was it which the apostle apprehended them to be in danger of? I answer, It was total and final apostasy. The truth of this proposition will fully appear by considering, first, what the apostle apprehended they were in danger of falling from. And, 1. He supposed them in danger of falling from divine, gospel illumination. 2. From tasting the heavenly gift. 3. From partaking of the Holy Ghost. 4. From tasting the

---

* See the chapter on Justification, in the Necessary Doctrine and Erudition for any Christian Man. ‡ Heylyn on the place. § See Dutch Annot.

good word of God. And, 5. From tasting the powers of the world to come. Add to this, secondly, the consideration of the effects and consequences of this falling. And, 1. The apostates are said, ἀνασαυρῖν, to crucify Christ a second time; and παραδειγματίζειν, to inflict open punishment on him: and, as Dr. *Hammond* has observed, "That "must need include renouncing and deny- "ing of Christ, the looking on him as such "as the Jews pretended him to be when "they crucified him, that is, an impostor §." *Beza* saith, "They that crucify him again, "make him a mocking-stock to all the "world, and that to their own destruction, as "*Julian* the apostate did*." And in King "*Edward* the Sixth's Bible it is, "They "which are apostates, and sin against the "Holy Ghost, hate Christ, crucify and "mock him, but to their own destruction, "and therefore fall into desparation, and "cannot repent †." The 2d effect would be, that the apostates would render it, ἀδύνατον, impossible for them to repent; of

conse

---

§ See Dr. Hammond on the place, Note *(a)*.
* Beza on the place. † Note on the Passage.

sequence their forgiveness would be rendered as impossible; then, of course, their salvation must be rendered equally impossible, and their damnation equally sure. Hence it is, that the apostle compares them to the earth which drinketh in the rain that cometh oft upon it, yet beareth thorns and briars; on which account it is, first, rejected; secondly, it is nigh unto cursing; and, thirdly, whose end, (that is, the end of the apostate, who is compared to the earth) is to be burned. "The end of such unhappy creatures," says Dr. *Doddridge*, "SHALL BE EVERLASTING BURNING†." And *Grotius* speaking of this ground observes, "*Sentibus et tribulis re-*"*spondet contemptus religionis Christianæ;* "*maledicto herili damnatio; incendio pœna* "*gehennæ:*" the contempt of the Christian Religion answers to the thorns and thistles—damnation, to the proprietor's curse; and hell-torments to the burning of the field‖. Once more; The *Assembly of Divines*

† Family Expositor, vol. vi. p. 47. ‖ Grotius in loc

Divines say, "As the earth painfully tilled
"and plentifully watered is good for no
"thing but to be burnt, if inftead of good
"fruit it bringeth forth thorns and thiftles:
"fo thofe who have been plentifully wa-
"tered with many fweet fhowers of the
"word of God, and enriched with divers
"excellent graces, are good for nothing
"but to BURN IN HELL FOR EVERMORE*"
One Mr. *Thomas Moore*, in a book entitled,
"An explicit declaration of the Teftimony
"of Chrift," &c. faith, on this paffage,
"The briars and thorns here meant, appear
"in this epiftle to be a letting flip the
"things we have heard, and fo a neglect
"of the great falvation, and a liftening to
"the deceitfulnefs of fin, and fo a harden-
"ing our hearts againft the teachings of
"the grace of God, and allowing in our-
"felves any root of bitternefs, uncleannefs,
"or prophanenefs, and fo turning from
"him that fpeaks from heaven, through an
"unbelieving heart departing from the
"living God. And then a neglect of the
ordi-

* Afiembly's Annotations on the place.

"ordinances of Christ, and a forsaking the
"assemblies of the saints; and then cruci-
"fying to themselves the Son of God
"afresh, and putting him to an open shame.
"And so when fallen from such a faith, by
"the Oracles of God fastened on such a
"foundation, and affording such princi-
"ples; they have trodden under foot the
"Son of God; and have counted the blood
"of the covenant wherewith they were
"sanctified, as an unholy thing, and have
"done despite to the Spirit of grace. These
"are briars and thorns; and these not re-
"penting, but continuing thus crucifying
"Christ, &c. even themselves are briars
"and thorns, nigh to cursing, being reject-
"ed, and their end is to be burned: and
"this justly and deservedly. Because of
"the truth, goodness, and riches of the
"faith, taught by such divine oracles, and
"brought on such a foundation; affording
"such principles, sweet experiences, and
"blessed hope, all so watered from heaven;
"as in others brought forth meet fruits;
"but the rewarding evil for good have so
"foully

"foully departed; and continue contemn-
"ing, and bring forth briars and thorns, till
"they" [themselves] "become briars and
"thorns: so that even in this demonstra-
"tion of the equity, justness, and holiness
"of God's proceeding, the faith they fell
"from, and that others abiding in, are
"found fruitful, and exhorted to abide,
"appears to be true, and of the right
"kind‖." From all that has been said, I conclude, that the falling away here spoken of, is nothing less than TOTAL and FINAL APOSTASY.

Before I dismiss this passage, I shall add a few testimonies to shew that learned and pious Calvinists as well as Arminians declare, that it is *total* and *final* apostasy which is spoken of in this passage. So *Diodati*: Those who "*fall away*—not by some par-
"ticular sin of human frailty, but by an
"ENTIRE and voluntary APOSTASY and
"renouncing of the faith, do return to their
"state of spiritual death, and TOTAL SE-
"PARATION FROM GOD, as they were
                                "before

‖ See the above Declaration, &c. p. 599.

"before their vocation.—He [the apostle]
"shews the IMPOSSIBILITY OF SUCH APOS-
"TATES' REPENTANCE, for their killing
"Christ maliciously*." So the author of
Critica Sacra, "If they shall fall away—
"ALTOGETHER, TOTALLY; *prolapsi, id
"est, prorsus lapsi.* Anselm. *Notat uni-
"versalem ab evangelio defectionem.* CALVIN.
"This place must be understood of a wil-
"ful malicious apostasy§." Dr. *Doddridge's*
paraphrase is, "If they TOTALLY fall
"away;" and he observes in his Note,
that "It is *certain* the words, fall away,
"MUST be understood thus; or it would
"prove, contrary to the plainest fact, that
"it is impossible to recover Christians who
"have fallen into great and wilful sins†."
D. *Dickson*, professor of Divinity in the
University of Glasgow, saith, The apostle
"presupposeth, except they study to make
"progress, they shall go backward: and
"that going backwards, tendeth to aposta-
"sy: and that voluntary and compleat
"apostasy from known truth doth harden
the

* See Diodati on the place. ‖ Leigh on the place.
† Family Expositor.

"the heart from repentance, and cutteth "off a man from mercy*." The learned *Trapp* expounds it thus: "If they shall fall "away—TOTALLY and FINALLY, as Judas "and Julian did‖." The *Assembly of Divines*, on chap. vi. verse 4. say, that "The "apostle observing that the Hebrews were "ready to revolt from the Christian faith, "into Judaism, and by little and little to "fall into the unpardonable sin which he "here describes, labours to keep them "from both: first by manifesting the dan- "ger of such a relapse†." Again, on verse 6. they say, "*Fall away*—that is, by uni- "versal apostasy, into Judaism, or Pagan- "ism, maliciously and despitefully con- "temning and persecuting the faith of "Christ; of whose truth they were con- "vinced in their consciences by the Holy "Ghost§." Bishop *Fell*, on chap vi. verse 6. says, "The apostle speaks of an uni- "versal apostasy from Christianity back to "Judaism‡." Mr. *Sam. Clark*, on those words,

* See Dickson on the place. ‖ Trapp's Comment, page 374. † Assembly's Comment. § Ibid. ‡ Fell on the place.

words, For it is impossible, &c. says, "It concerns you to make some progress in Christianity, because the neglect thereof makes way for apostasy*." The continuators of *Pool*, say, "The foregoing counsel the Spirit enforceth on the Hebrews, from the danger of apostasy, to which the neglect of it doth dispose them, and the terrifying consequences of it, from verse 4. to 9. We must go on to perfection unless we will DRAW BACK TO PERDITION; so he bespeaks them: you have been sluggish and dull, and going backward already; lest you grow worse, stir up yourselves; if you neglect it, YOU ARE IN DANGER OF UTTERLY FALLING AWAY§." The learned *Beza* saith on the place, "He [the apostle] addeth a most sharp threatning of the CERTAIN DESTRUCTION that shall come to them who fall from GOD and his religion." Again: "He [the apostle] speaketh of a general backsliding, and such as do ALTOGETHER "FALL

---

* Clark on the place. § Pool on the place.

" FALL AWAY FROM THE FAITH†." *Gomarus*, and *Jacobus Capellus*, on the place, (as quoted by *Pool*) tell us that the sense of it is, " *Desinite retrocedere, ne abducemini in* " *defectionem ac ruinam prorsus insanabilem :*" Cease to draw back, lest you FALL INTO " APOSTASY, and into a DESTRUCTION AL-" TOGETHER WITHOUT REMEDY*." *Calvin* says on these words, of the apostles, If they " fall away, &c. that the persons spoken " of are not men, " *qui aliqua in parte* " *Deum offendunt, sed qui ejus gratiâ se peni-* " *tus abdicant,*" who are guilty of some partial offence before GOD; but who totally " abdicate or abandon his grace‡. *Wilson*, author of the Christian Dictionary, expounds To fall away, " By universal apostasy into " Judaism or Paganism, maliciously and " despitefully contemning, persecuting, or " opposing the faith of Christ; of whose " truth they are convinced in their consci- " ences by the Holy Ghost§." In the Book of Homilies we are told, that " In the sixth " and tenth chapters of the epistle to the
" Hebrews,

---

† Beza in loc. * Synop. Crit. ii. loc. ‡ Calv. in loc.
§ Christian Dictionary on the place.

"Hebrews," the apostle is speaking "of The FINAL falling away from Christ and his gospel, which is a sin against the Holy Ghost, that shall never be forgiven, because that they do UTTERLY forsake the known truth, do hate Christ and his word, they do crucify and mock him, (but to their utter destruction) and therefore fall into desperation, and cannot repent[*]."

But it may be said, "The apostasy here spoken of by the apostle, is not to be understood of true believers; but of hypocrites and false professors." To this I answer, first, It has already been demonstrated that the persons spoken of were true believers, and genuine Christians. Secondly, To suppose them to be any other than true believers, is absurd and contradictory. For if they were only hypocrites and carnal professors, they never properly stood, and therefore could not fall. Again, if they were only carnal hypocrites, they had no genuine repentance; and therefore, to talk

---

[*] First part of the Hom. on Repentance.

of RENEWING them *again* to that which they never had, is abfurd with a witnefs! If it is faid, that "They had common "grace, from which they might fall;" then I afk, Would hypocrites, by falling from this *common*, unfaving grace, crucify unto themfelves the Son of God afrefh, and put him to an open fhame? And would they, by falling from this counterfeit grace, be rejected, and nigh unto curfing, and at laft be burned? And is the fin of falling from fuch falfe, ineffectual grace, fo aggravated, that it is impoffible to renew unto repenance thofe who have once been guilty of it?

Again, it may be objected farther, that the apoftle fays, verfe 9. "But, beloved, we are perfuaded better things of you, and things that accompany falvation, though we fpeak thus." True: but then the queftion is, What does he mean? It is impoffible he fhould mean, We have a full, abfolute perfuafion, that you cannot let this great falvation flip; that you cannot poffibly let go the confidence and the rejoicing of of the hope; that you cannot harden your hearts as in the provocation; that you are incapable of an evil heart of unbelief in departing from the living GOD, that you cannot be hardened through the deceitfulness of sin, or fall through unbelief. Had this been his meaning, how came he to suppose that they were in danger of these evils, and to write a whole epistle to prevent their falling into them? What! did an inspired apostle caution them against letting the great salvation slip, while he was absolutely persuaded that they could not do it! Did he, in the most solemn manner, warn them not to depart from the living God, while he had an absolute persuasion that it was impossible? 'Tis absurd and impious once to imagine it. No: if the apostle (I will not say was inspired; but if he) was in his senses, he did not write this verse on purpose to contradict all the rest of the epistle.

But what then did he mean? I answer, that he was persuaded, first, that these Hebrews were not THEN of the number abovementioned; that is, that they were not apostates

apostates AT THAT TIME; and, secondly, that he hoped, or believed, IN A JUDGMENT OF CHARITY, that they never would.

That this matter may be set in a clear light, let it be observed, 1. That before the writing of this epistle, great numbers of the converted Hebrews had already totally apostatized from Christ and his gospel: and 2. that many of those who were not yet thus fallen, began to abate in their attachment to Christ, and were in danger of imitating their brethren, by a like total apostasy.

Now, as the awful threatnings made use of in the preceding verses were intended to alarm their fears, and thereby to prevent their ruin, the apostle was apprehensive that some of them might make a wrong use thereof, by concluding that he thought their case already desperate; and that, because they had begun to decline, he thought, that by so doing, they had crucified unto themselves the Son of GOD afresh, and put him to an open shame. and that, therefore, he thought they were the persons who were incapable of repentance, and who resembled

the

the earth which was rejected, and nigh unto cursing, whose end was to be burned.

To prevent, or remove this mistake, the apostle added these words, " Beloved, we are persuaded better things of you, and things which accompany salvation, though we speak thus." As if he had said, Though we speak with such seeming severity, and lay before you such dreadful considerations; you must not hence conclude that we look upon you AS ALREADY in that dreadful condition. For we are persuaded better things of you; namely, that, AT PRESENT you are in a state of salvation, and in the way to the full and eternal enjoyment of it, and the great love we have for you gives us a *charitable persuasion*, or *hope*, that you will continue therein. Nevertheless, as we see you exposed to great dangers, we think it our duty to warn you in the most solemn manner.

An excellent commentator who wrote on this epistle about the year 1646, and who is strongly recommended by Mr. *John Downame*, expounds this passage thus; " I am persuaded that you are YET in that
" state

" ſtate that ye may be ſaved, if ye have a
" will to it." Mr *Weſley*'s expoſition is,
" We are perſuaded you are now ſaved
" from your ſins: and that ye have that
" faith, love, and holineſs which leads to
" final ſalvation, though we ſpeak thus to
" warn you, leſt you ſhould *fall* from your
" preſent ſteadfaſtneſs.*" Profeſſor *Dickſon*
" tells us that the apoſtle " MITIGATETH
" HIS THREATNING, for fear of hurting
" their faith§." The learned *Beza* ſaith,
" He [the apoſtle] MITIGATETH and AS-
" SUAGETH all that ſharpneſs, HOPING
" better of them to whom he writeth.‡"
Dr. *Doddridge*'s paraphraſe is, " We have
" this *chearful expectation* concerning you,
" though we think ourſelves obliged thus
" to ſpeak; that nothing may be wanting
" to guard you againſt the greateſt dan-
" ger†." The Calvinian Aſſembly expound
the paſſage thus: " But beloved——To
" *moderate and ſweeten* his former harſh-
" neſs, here he ſhews his good opinion
" which he had of the Hebrews, and to
" comfort

* See *Weſley* on the place. § *Dickſon* on the place.
‡ *Beza* in loc. † *Pool*'s Expoſitor.

"comfort them, by giving them assurance
"of God's mercy in rewarding them, *if*
"they continue steadfast in their profession.
"See chap. x. 39*."—"*Temperat austeri-
"tatem præcedentium verborum*," says *Eras-
mus*‡: the apostle tempers here the severity of the preceding expressions. Mr.
Henry saith, "The apostle having applied
"himself to the fears of these Hebrews,
"for the exciting their diligence, and pre-
"venting their APOSTASY, now proceeds
"to apply himself to their hopes, and can-
"didly declares the *good hope*," (not the
absolute persuasion) "he had concerning
"them, that they would persevere; and
"proposes to them the great encouragement
"they had in the way of their duty§."
Mr. *Thomas More* saith, "And now in
"his supposition he set forth before them
"the heinousness of the sin and danger of
"such *departing* and *falling away*; compar-
"ing such transgressions and transgressors,
"to briars and thorns, whose end is to be
"burned, he *mollifies* the harshness of his
"sentence

* Assembly's Annot. ‡ Erasm. in loc. § Henry on the place.

" sentence in respect of them, and saith, We
" are persuaded better things of you, and
" things that accompany salvation, though
" we thus speak; which plainly shews the
" better things to be better than thorns and
" briars, which tended to damnation; and
" it shews also that his speech in the warn-
" ing was directed to Them; else they
" needed not to be *mollified* with, Though
" we thus speak. Surely none would fancy
" the apostle to warn the Hebrews, by
" speaking at such a rate as this! There is
" a rock of stability, on which whoever
" once believeth"—" can no more fall off
" —and you are upon that rock, &c. Hold
" fast therefore your confidence; take heed
" lest any of you fall through an evil heart
" of unbelief: and give us leave to fear
" lest any of you come short; for there is
" an unstable rock, on which, not you, but
" some others are built. And they that are
" built on that rock of instability, if they
" abide, they perish; if they fall, they can
" no more rise*." " By these words," say
the

---

* More's Works, page 613.

the Dutch Annotators, " the apostle *molli-*
"*fies* the former threatning, and declares
" in that which follows, why he sets before
" them the grievous punishment of *apostates*,
" namely, not that he held them to be such,
" but to warn them, and to exhort them
" to hold fast to the doctrine of the gos-
" pel, and to God's promises*." Father
Quesnel's remark is, " Ill does that person
" understand the art of gaining upon the
" minds of men, who is always full of
" reproaches and invectives. If we find
" them dejected by the dread of damna-
" tion, and by our upbraiding them with
" their impenitency, we must raise their
" spirits by marks of our ESTEEM and
" HOPE‖."

From all that hath been said, we learn,
1. That they are not different persons who
are spoken of in this, and the preceding
verses, but one and the same. 2. That all
that is intended in this verse is, to *soften*
the seeming severity of the former remarks,
lest the Hebrews, instead of being stirred
up

* See Dutch Annotations on the place.   ‖ Quesnel's
New Testament on the place.

up to godly jealousy, by what was said, should abandon themselves to despair. Now of this interpretation I observe two things, 1. It preserves, (yea, and is absolutely necessary to preserve) the connexion and coherence of the place. And, 2. That on this account it is, that the most learned and candid among the calvinian writers are constrained to insert it.

9. The next proof that falling away was the evil intended by the apostle, we have in verse 11. of this chapter. "And we desire that every one of you do shew the same diligence to the full assurance of hope unto the end." On this passage, I observe, That *perseverance* to the end was that which the apostle had still in view: therefore the evil he supposed them to be in danger of was that of APOSTASY, or of not persevering to the end. And it is very observable, with what prudence the apostle proceeds in labouring to prevent the apostasy of these Hebrews. From the 4th to the 8th verse, he uses an argument of great terror, to alarm their fears. Then, lest this should terrify them too

too much, in the 9th and 10th verses, he lifts them up by declaring that he was perfuaded better things of them. " For God is not unrighteous, fays he, to forget your works and labour of love, which ye have fhewed towards his name, in that ye have miniftered to the faints, and do minifter. " And now again," fays a learned author, " left they fhould be too confident of them-
" felves—and flatter themfelves with an in-
" fallible hope of falvation, he fhews them
" their wants, that being thus reduced to a
" temper, that they might not defpair of
" falvation, nor prefume of it." And that they might not thus prefume, We defire, faid the apoftle, that every one of you may fhew the fame diligence, that you have formerly fhewn, and ftill are fhewing, unto the full affurance of hope unto the end: that is, according to Dr. *Doddridge*, " in
" order to ESTABLISH the full affurance of
" your hope, even unto the end of your
" Chriftian courfe‡:" For, according to Father *Quefnel*, " It is not fo much good
" works, as PERSEVERANCE in them, which
  " affures

‡ See Family Expofitor.

"assures our hope*."—These words, unto the end, may be applied, first, unto the diligence which the apostle recommends; and then the meaning is, that he desired the Hebrews might continue this unto the end; which supposes that there was a possibility of their not doing it. Or, secondly, they may be applied to the full assurance of hope; and then the meaning is, that they ought to keep up their former diligence that this full assurance might continue to the end; which supposes it possible for it not to continue: or which is the same, that they might apostatize from it.

10. The next passage which I shall produce in proof of the point is, chap. x. verse 23. "Let us hold fast the profession of our ελπιδος, hope, without wavering." The hope here spoken of was, undoubtedly, the hope of everlasting life. And the profession of it, was that which the Hebrews had first made at their baptism, and continued to make to the time the apostle wrote this epistle.

* Quesnel's New Test. on the place.

epistle. Now, when he exhorted them to hold fast this *profession*, he tacitly acknowledged that there was a possibility of their *not* holding it fast; or, in other words, of their falling away from it. And in supposing this, he supposed there was a possibility of their not holding fast the *practice* which was the effect of their profession. And then that there was a possibility of their not holding fast the *hope* itself. For it is certain, that when the profession, &c. of this hope was gone, the hope itself could not continue.—Hence Mr. *Baxter's* comment is, " Let us, against all subtle, de-
" ceitful adversaries, against all cruel perse-
" cutors, under all trials and sufferings,
" HOLD FAST both our *hope* and *faith*, and
" the open PROFESSION of it[*]." The Continuators of *Pool* expound the words thus: " Let us therefore PERSEVERE in
" the FAITH and HOPE of him; really,
" actually, STEADFASTLY RETAINING, with
" all our might and power, whatsoever
" insinuations may be used to entice us, or

[*] Baxter on the place.

"violence of persecution to force us from
"it, RETAINING it still in our mind, will,
"affections and operations‡." Mr. *Henry*
saith, "Our spiritual enemies will do
"what they can to *wrest our faith*, and
"*hope*, and *holiness*, and *comfort*, OUT OF
"OUR HANDS; but we must HOLD FAST
"our religion as our best treasure. The
"manner how we must do this, is, without
"wavering, without doubting, without dis-
"puting, without dallying with tempta-
"tion to apostasy"—"They that begin to
"waver in matters of Christian faith and
"practice, ARE IN DANGER OF FALLING
"AWAY†." The Dutch Annotators say,
"Let us hold fast, that is, STEADFASTLY
"RETAIN, without turning from it, or be-
"ing seduced from it, the unwavering
"profession of hope: namely, WHICH IS
"IN US‖." This passage then is another
demonstration that the apostle's caution is
against APOSTASY.

11. Again, verse 25. "Not forsaking
the assembling of ourselves together, as the
manner

---
‡ Pool's Comment. † Henry's Comment. on the place. ‖ Dutch Annot. on the place.

manner of some is: but exhorting one another, and so much the more as ye see the day approaching." It is certain that the assemblies here spoken of, were the public and private assemblies of the Christian church. Now when the apostle said to these Hebrews, " Not forsaking the assembling of yourselves together, as the manner of some is," he in effect declared, 1. That some of them had already done this. And, 2. That he saw that those to whom he wrote the epistle were in danger of following their bad example. This is evident from the advice he here gives them, 1. Negatively: not to forsake these assemblies. 2. Affirmatively: but to exhort one another, " To " *perseverance* in the faith," says Dr. *Whitby*||. And so much the more as ye see the day approaching, which will put an end to all your present troubles. *Estius* on the place observes, that the apostle exhorts the Hebrews, " *Ne ecclesiam deserant per schis-* " *ma, aut apostasiam, ad quam Hebræi pro-* " *clives erant. Sic Latini ferè accipiunt**.

" Not

|| See Whitby on the place. * Syn. Crit. in. loc.

Not to forsake the church by schism or APOSTASY, to which the Hebrews were inclined. "this is, said he, the almost "GENERAL SENTIMENT OF THE LATIN "FATHERS." Mr. *Henry* saith, "We "have the means prescribed for preventing "our APOSTASY, and promoting our fide- "lity and PERSEVERANCE, ver. 24, 25, &c." Again: "There were in the apostles time, "and should be in every age, Christian "assemblies for the worship of GOD, and "for mutual edification. And it seems, "even in those times there were some who "forsook these assemblies, and so began to "apostatize from religion itself. The com- "munion of saints is a great help and pri- "vilege, and a good means of steadiness "and *perseverance*§." Again: "After "having mentioned these means of estab- "lishment, the apostle proceeds, in the "close of the chapter, to enforce his "exhortations TO PERSEVERANCE, and "AGAINST APOSTASY, by many very "weighty considerations, ver. 26, 27, &c‖."

The

---

§ Henry on the place. ‖ Ibid.

The calvinian *Dickson's* remark is, "That mutual edification of Christians among themselves"—"is a special help to *constancy* in true religion, and a preservative against APOSTASY†:" which abundantly shews, that, according to the judgment of this learned Calvinist, APOSTASY was the evil which the apostle was labouring to prevent.

12. The next proof of the business in hand we have in the 26th and following verses. "For if we sin wilfully, after that we have received the knowledge of the truth, there remaineth no more sacrifice for sin: verse 27. But a certain fearful looking for of judgment and fiery indignation, which shall devour the adversaries. Verse 28. He that despised Moses' law died without mercy under two or three witnesses: verse 29. of how much sorer punishment, suppose ye, shall he be thought worthy, who hath trodden underfoot the Son of God, and hath counted the blood of the covenant wherewith he was sanctified, an

† Dickson on the place.

unholy thing, and hath done despite unto the Spirit of grace."

Observe, 1. The sin here spoken of is, a wilful FALLING AWAY. This is evident, first, from hence, it is said to be done, ἑκουσίως, wilfully. The Geneva translation renders it, *Scientes et volentes*, wittingly and willingly. They who thus sinned, did it, not through ignorance, as carnal and unenlightened people often do; but they did it with their eyes quite open. *Calvin* saith, " *Non lo-*
" *quitur de particularibus lapsibus, sed de*
" *universali defectione, qua illi ultro, scientes,*
" *et volentes, se ab ecclesiæ societate et a*
" *Christo alienabant atque abducabant:*"—
He [the apostle] does not speak of particular falls; but of an *universal defection*, by which they, of their own accord, knowingly, and willingly, left the society of the church, and renounced THEIR INTEREST IN CHRIST.† So *Baxter*· " The dreadful
" case of *apostates* must deter you: for if you
" WILFULLY forsake *Christ* and *Christianity*, after you have received the knowledge
" of

† Calvin in loc.

" of the truth of it, BY THE SPIRIT*," &c. Secondly, it is said to be done after receiving, επιγνωσει της αληθειας, the acknowledgment of the truth: after they had, not only heard the truth; but after they had inwardly experienced it, and had outwardly acknowledged it. The continuators of *Pool*, on these words say, " Who sinneth
" at a higher rate than a Jew against *Moses*'s
" law, being an APOSTATE from the gos-
" pel, a revolter from, and a rebel against
" it§." The Dutch Annotators say, " For
" if we sin wilfully—that is, wilfully FALL
" AWAY FROM THIS FAITH, which the
" apostle hath here described, as hereafter
" in verse 29. this sin is more largely de-
" clared, which the apostle also, as hereto-
" fore, chap. vi. verse 6. calleth a falling
" away. He speaketh not here, then, of
" every kind of sin or falling away; but of
" that sin which Christ calleth the blasphe-
" my against the Holy Ghost‡.

Observe,

---

* Baxter on the place.   § Pool's Comment.
‡ Dutch Annot. on the place.

Obſerve, 2. That it is TOTAL AND FINAL APOSTASY which is here ſpoken of. This is evident, firſt, from thoſe effects of this ſin which reſpect GOD and his grace. 1. He who hath thus ſinned, hath trodden underfoot the Son of GOD: that is, he hath treated him in the moſt contemptuous manner, as if he were dung, and droſs. *Theophylact, Ambroſe,* and *Primaſius,* expound καταπατεω, "contemn and deſpiſe Chriſt:" and the author of Critica Sacra renders it "Extremity of contempt." 2. He hath counted the blood of the covenant, wherewith he was ſanctified, an unholy, κοινον, an unclean thing. Dr. *Doddridge's* paraphraſe is, "a common or an unclean thing, like "the blood of a malefactor juſtly executed "for his crimes†." *Pool* quotes *Gomarus, Eſtius, Menochius, Ribera,* and *Grotius,* as ſaying that this paſſage belongs, "*Ad apoſtatam, qui eo ſanctificatus dicitur,* "*i. e. redemptus, emundatus a peccatis, &c.* "*a vitiis purgatus, ſanctuſque factus, remiſſi-* "*onem peccatorum, et ſanctificationem conſe-* "*cutus.*"

† See Doddridge on the place.

" *cutus,*" to an APOSTATE, who on that account is said to have been sanctified, i. e. redeemed, cleansed from his sins, &c. made pure from his vices, and holy; having obtained remission of sins, and sanctification‖. And the Continuators of *Pool* tell us that, " Ευ ω ηγιασθη, *in,* or *by* which he was sanc-" tified, IS BY MOST interpreters referred " to the APOSTATES‡."—When the apostle said that the apostate *counted* the blood of the covenant a common, unclean, or an unholy thing, he meant, that the apostate's behaviour was exactly such as if he had counted it so. 3. He hath done despite to the Spirit of Grace. That *is,* he hath treated that good Spirit, which was graciously bestowed on him, for gracious purposes, as if he was a most vile and hateful enemy. *Diodati* expounds it thus, " Do " despite—by secret or open blasphemies, " with thoughts, deeds, and words, against " GOD's truth which hath been revealed " unto him, and the certainty whereof hath " been REVEALED IN HIS HEART BY THE
" HOLY

‖ Syn. Crit. in loc.   ‡ Pool's Comment.

"Holy Ghost§." Dr. *Whitby* says, "To do despite unto the Spirit of grace, cannot well signify less than that which our Lord stiles the sin against the Holy Ghost, which men cannot commit, and in their hearts be Christians*." *Grotius* says, "*Vides hic etiam eos qui Spiritum acceperant, qui nisi justificatis non dabatur, defectores fieri posset* †:" You see here also, that those *who had received the Spirit,* which was not given to any *but the justified,* may become APOSTATES. The continuators of *Pool* expound the words thus: "Injuring, wronging, despising, greatly grieving, not a creature, but GOD the Spirit, the quickening Spirit of dead sinners, who fits them for union with GOD, and in order to it uniteth them to Christ and his body, and animateth them; who graciously communicated to THESE APOSTATES the knowledge natural and SUPERNATURAL, which THEY HAD and ABUSED ‖."

Again; that it is TOTAL and FINAL apostasy which is here spoken of, is evident,

secondly,

---

§ Diodati on the place
† Grotius in loc.
* Whitby on the place.
‖ Pool's Comment.

secondly, from the consequences of it which relate to the apostate himself. These are, 1. That God looks on the apostate as an adversary. This is evident from verse 27th. where he is expressly called an adversary. He had acted the part of an adversary in treading under foot the Son of God, in counting the blood of the covenant an unholy thing, and in doing despite unto the Spirit of grace: and, therefore, God judged of him according to what he was. 2. There remained no more sacrifice for his sins. As he had rejected, yea trampled on that sacrifice which God had provided for him; so God, in righteous judgment, determined that he should have no other. 3. Instead of having another sacrifice, a fiery indignation was provided to devour him. 4. This indignation was to come upon him in a forer manner than that which came on those who despised the law of Moses, and who died without mercy. I therefore conclude upon the whole, that the apostle could not here intend any thing less than TOTAL AND FINAL APOSTASY.

And

And the truth of this conclusion is so evident, that the most learned Calvinists, as well as Arminians have been constrained to acknowledge it. *Pool* quotes not only *Erasmus*, but *Beza* also, and other divines, who say that the apostle speaks, "*De pec-* "*cato apostasiæ a fide et religione Christianá,* "*quo quis ex professo, et in universum resilit* "*a Christo,*" of the sin of APOSTASY from the faith, and the Christian religion, whereby a man openly, and TOTALLY falls back from Christ*. Mr. *Sam. Clark*, on the place faith, " It concerns us to use all means to " PERSEVERE, because APOSTASY is so " dangerous‡." King *Edward*'s Bible hath it, For if we sin wilfully—" That is, for- " sake JESUS CHRIST, as *Judas, Saul, Arius,* " *Julian* the APOSTATE did†." The *Assembly of Divines* say, " The apostle doth " speak here, not of all kinds of wilful " sin, or falling away; but only of that " which our Lord CHRIST calleth blasphe- " my against the Holy Ghost§." So *Diodati*:
" I

---

* Syn. Crit. in loc. ‡ Clark's Comment.
† Note on the place. § Assembly's Annotations.

"I exhort you to take heed of the first
"degrees of impiety, for by them YOU
"MAY FALL INTO THE EXTREME, WHICH
"IS THE IRREMISSIBLE SIN AGAINST THE
"HOLY GHOST." He adds on the word,
"wilfully, by a TOTAL APOSTACY and ex-
"tinction of the Holy Ghost, done purpose-
"ly and through malice with delight*."
To the same purpose are the words of
Professor *Dickson*, on verse 29. "Ano-
"ther motive to constancy in the truth of
"religion, taken from the fearful case of
"WILFUL APOSTATES, who sinning the
"sin against the Holy Ghost are secluded,
"FOR EVER, from mercy. I say, the sin
"against the Holy Ghost; because we shall
"find the sin here described, not to be any
"particular sin against the law, but against
"the gospel: not against some point of
"truth, but against Christ's whole doc-
"trine: not of infirmity, but wilfulness.
"not of rashness, but of deliberation, wit-
"tingly and willingly: not of ignorance,
"but after illumination, and profession:
"such as Jews turned Christians, revolting
"from

* Diodati on the place.

"from christianity, back again to their
"former hostility against Christ, did com-
"mit*." By sinning wilfully, Dr. *Gill*
says, "The apostle intends a TOTAL APOS-
"TASY from the truth, against light and
"evidence, joined with obstinacy‡." Dr.
Doddridge on these words, trodden under foot the son of GOD, says, "It ap-
"pears to me, that this is a description of
"a case that could only occur, when what
"was properly the sin against the Holy
"Ghost was committed∥." So the learned
Trapp: "For if we sin wilfully against the
"grace of the gospel, despising and de-
"spiting it, as those do that fall into the
"unpardonable sin§," &c. I shall conclude
this point with the words of Dr. *Whitby*.
"They so sinned that there remained no
"more sacrifice for sin; but a fearful
"looking for of judgment and fiery indig-
"nation, and so as to do despite to the spi-
"rit of grace, by rejecting him as a lying
"spirit, and his gifts and miracles as illu-
"sions, and so were guilty of the sin
"against

---

* Dickson on the place.   ‡ Gill on the place
∥ Doddridge on the place.   § Trapp on the place.

" against the Holy Ghost, fell TOTALLY
" and FINALLY, is so exceeding evident,
" that I know of none who ever ventured
" to deny it*."

13. The next passage which shews that neglecting to persevere was the evil the apostle apprehended these Hebrews to be in danger of, is the 35th verse of this same chapter. " Cast not away therefore, your confidence, which hath great recompence of reward." By confidence, the apostle intended faith in Christ, and liberty of freely confessing it. And that this confidence was a true and genuine one, appears from hence, that it had a great recompence of reward. Nevertheless, these Hebrews could CAST IT AWAY, otherwise the apostle would not have supposed they could, by bidding them not do it. The continuators of *Pool* say, that this passage " In-
" troduceth the last direction for helping
" on their *perseverance* in christianity:" and add, that " Μη αποβαλλητε, denieth all de-
" grees

* Whitby on the five points, page 407.

"gices of APOSTASY†." *Jacobus Capel-lus* and *Beza* (as quoted by *Pool*) say, *Ne igitur (cum tam horrendum sit desertorum exitium, &c.) abjicite, vel jacturam facite rei tam pretiosæ*: Since the destruction of APOSTATES is so horrible, &c. do not cast away, do not throw over-board so precious a thing [as your confidence, &c. is]‡.

14. Again, verse 38. Now the just shall live by faith; but if any man draw back, my soul shall have no pleasure in him. The original word, υποστειληται, is a military term, taken from soldiers who draw back out of their place, and in whom their captain has no delight. Therefore the learned *Trapp* renders it, "Steal from their "colours, run away from their captain§." Dr. *Whitby* hath justly observed, that "Dr. "*Hammond* hath shewed from *Phavorinus*, "that this word signifies, to draw back, re-"fuse, and fly from a thing‖." *Aretius* renders Και εαν υποστειληται, *Et si subductus fuerit:*

---

† Pool's comment on the place. ‡ Ibid.
§ See Trapp on the place ‖ Whitby on the place.

fuerit: and expounds it, *Ostendunt autem judicium Domini contra apostasiam, et cordis pertinaciam seu rebellionem, q. d. rebellio sine morâ separat ab amore Dei, ex amicis hostes facit, ex patre Deo inimicum et vindicem facit**. the meaning of which is, That *apostasy* and rebellion presently separate from the love of God: of friends make men enemies, and make God an enemy and an avenger, who was a father. The Dutch annotators say, " And if (any " one) withdraw [namely, from his faith " and patient expectation, by apostasy, and " denial of Christ and his truth] my soul " hath no pleasure in him†." The Assembly of Divines say, " Draw back—from " their faith and patient expectation, by " FALLING AWAY and denying Christ and " his truth‡." It is therefore certain that the apostle was here speaking of falling away.—But what kind of falling was it? I answer, TOTAL AND FINAL APOSTASY. That it was total apostasy appears from

---

* See Aretius in loc.
† Dutch Annot. on the place.
‡ Assembly's Annotations.

hence, God says, " My soul shall have no pleasure, ουκ ευδοκει, in him. Ουκ ευδοκειν, is an Hebraism, says *Suicerus*, in which, as in many other places, more is intended than expressed; and is an expression of the strongest aversion and abhorrence*. So the calvinian author of Critica Sacra says, " More is meant than spoken, after a He-
" brew manner of speech, as though he
" should say, I *abhor* all those that fall
" away through unbelief†." The renowned *John Goodwin* expounds it thus: " My soul
" shall have no pleasure in him, *i. e.* (ac-
" cording to the import of the Hebraism),
" my soul shall HATE OR ABHOR HIM TO
" THE DEATH‡." Now, if God has NO pleasure in such a one, but does hate or abhor him to the death, it must be, because he is fallen into *total* apostasy. The continuators of *Pool* say, that " the Hebrew word
" here translated υποστειληται, is variously
" rendered, as elated like a bubble, lifted
" up, making pride and unbelief to be the
" sins threatened here; and the proper sense
" of

---

* Suicerus Theus. Fecl.   † Leigh on the place.
‡ See Redem. Redeemed, page 290.

"of the word here ufed, is, for fear, or
"floth to withdraw, or leave their ftand-
"ing; fo that the meaning in both" (the
Hebrew and Greek words), "amounts to
"this, If any, out of the pride of their
"heart, will not depend on Chrift's righ-
"teoufnefs, as the Jews would not, or out
"of fear and fluggifhnefs will not hold
"out, but withdraw themfelves in time of
"perfecution, from their faith and confi-
"dence in Chrift, profeffed, fhrinking
"through fear, or lofing it through floth,
"or forfaking it by treachery, either gra-
"dually or totally, confiding in themfelves,
"and fo defpifing God, reject him, and
"draw away from him—God himfelf will
"be fo far from taking any pleafure or de-
"light in fuch a foul, or vouchfafe it any
"joy or life, that his very foul abhors it,
"is highly difpleafed with its fin, and
"ABOMINATES ITS PERSON. In his dif-
"pleafure is mifery, death, and ETERNAL
"PERDITION*." So *Baxter*, "If any
"man forfake THIS FAITH, and its profef-

* Pool's Comment on the place.

"sion, either through fraud, flattery or fear of men, God will forsake him†." Father *Quesnel*'s remark is, "All the past is counted for nothing, unless PERSEVERANCE secures the future‡." Therefore *Baxter*, in another place saith, "If any man draw back, Christ saith, his soul shall have no pleasure in him. Even those that have endured the great fight of affliction, being reproached and made a gazing stock, and that have taken joyfully the spoiling of their goods, in assurance of a better and enduring substance, have yet need to be warned, that they cast not away their confidence, and draw back to perdition, and lose not the reward for want of patience and perseverance§." And that *final*, as well as total apostasy, is here intended, appears from hence, that the apostate is said to draw back unto ἀπωλειαν, *perdition* or *destruction*: yea, to that perdition or destruction which is opposed to the περιποιησιν ψυχης, to the saving,

† Baxter on the place. ‡ Quesnel's New Test. on the place. § See Epistle dedicatory to a book, entitled, The Right Method for a settled Peace of Conscience and Spiritual Comfort.

ing, delivering, or preserving of the soul.

But it may be said, "The person who is supposed to draw back, is not the same with him who lives by faith: he is only a hypocrite or carnal professor who draws back." To this I answer, What can a hypocrite or carnal professor draw back from? If he draws back at all, it must be either from that which is good, or else from that which is evil. If he draws back from that which is good, then he had goodness to draw back from, the carnal professor is in reality, no carnal professor:—Or if he had no goodness to draw back from, and so was in truth, a carnal professor, then, in this case, he drew back from that which he never had! If he draws back from that which is evil, would GOD have no pleasure in him on that account! or would GOD hate or abhor him to the death, as *Goodwin* hath it? and is this the way, viz. by drawing back from that which is evil, to involve himself in that perdition which is opposed to the saving of the soul!

But it may be objected farther, that "The apostle doth not say, if any of *you*,
"but

"but if any *man* draw back," &c. I answer, the original is και εαν υποστειληται, AND, or, BUT IF HE (that is, the juft man that liveth by faith,) " draw back." Theophylact fays,—Εαν υποςειληται ο δικαιος, τυ]εςιν, αμφιβολιαν τινα παθη και διςαγμον· η το υποςειληται, αν]ι τε υπο]απεινωθη τοις πειραςμοις. If the juft man fhall draw back; that is, if he fhall be doubtful, or hefitate, or give place to temptation*. Mr. *Wefley* renders it, " If, " ο δικαιος, the juft man that lives by faith " (fo the expreffion neceffarily implies, " there being no other nominative to the " verb,) draws back, my foul fhall have " no pleafure in him†." Dr. *Whitby* renders εαν υποςειληται, " If HE draws back;" " and obferves that it refers plainly to " the juft man who lives by faith‡." Dr. *Hammond*, after having examined the original words as they are found in this place in other parts of the New Teftament; and after having examined them as they are found in Heb. ii. verfe 4. according to the Septuagint, Hebrew, Chaldea, Arabic, the Targum,

---

* Theophyl. in loc. page 987. † Predeft. calmly calmly confidered, page 38, third edit. ‡ Whitby on the five points, page 408.

gum, &c. and after confidering the interpretation of *Phavorinus,* Rabbi *Tanchum, Ignatius,* and our English *Pocock,* obferves,—" And all this fets down the true notion "of the word in this place, thus. But if "HE that fhould live by his faith, fhall "cowardly withdraw himfelf from the "public worfhip of Chrift," &c. So again; "If—the juft, the Chriftian proves thus pu- "fillanimous, hangs back from the per- "formance of his duty; if by afflictions "he be difheartened and terrified, GOD's "foul hath no pleafure in him, he is ut- "terly rejected and difliked by GOD*." The learned and calvinian *Diodati* explains this drawing back as done by the juft man who lives by faith. "The juft," fays he, "Draw back—if HE depart from his belief "in me, if he becomes carelefs or difloyal "in following my vocation†," &c. Dr. *Heylin* fuppofes the fame, "The juft fhall "live by faith; but if HE draws back, re- "treats or deferts his poft, he fhall not be "approved by me‡." So *Calvin* renders it,

Juftus

---

* See Hammond on the place · note. † Diodati on the place. ‡ Heylin on the place.

"*Juſtus autem ex fide vivet: et ſi ſubductus fuerit, non oblectabitur,*" &c. that is, and if HE ſhall draw, or be drawn back, my ſoul, &c.* And ſo evident is this, that even Mr. *Kendal,* who wrote againſt Mr. *John Goodwin*'s Redemption Redeemed, ſays, "I "YIELD THAT ANY MAN IS NOT IN THE "TEXT†."

But it may be objected again, that "The "apoſtle, in the next verſe ſaith, We "are not of them who draw back unto "perdition: but of them that believe to "the ſaving of the ſoul." I anſwer, The apoſtle does ſay ſo. But then the queſtion is, what does he mean? It is impoſſible for him to mean, we are not of that ſort of people who CAN draw back unto perdition; but we are of that ſort who MUST believe to the ſaving of the ſoul. Had this been his meaning, how came he to write a whole epiſtle to warn and caution them not to draw back? How came he to caution them againſt letting this ſalvation ſlip? chap. ii. verſe 1. againſt hardening their hearts as in

the

---

* Calvin in loc.   † See Anſwer to Redemption Redeemed.

the provocation? chap. iii. verse 8.—against an evil heart of unbelief, in departing from the living God? verse 12.—against being hardened through the deceitfulness of sin? verse 13.—against falling through unbelief? chap. iv. verse 11.—against not holding fast their profession? verse 14.—against falling in such manner as to be incapable of being renewed again unto repentance? chap. vi. verse 4. 6.—against not being diligent to the end? verse 11.—against not holding fast their profession? chap. x. 23.—against forsaking the assembling of themselves together? verse 25 —against sinning wilfully after having received the knowledge of the truth? verse 26.—against casting away their confidence? verse 35.—against drawing back in such manner that God shall have no pleasure in them? verse 28.—To suppose that the apostle would send such a number of warnings and cautions to these Hebrews, and then tell them that they were not the persons to whom these cautions belonged, is to suppose that he wrote only for the sake of absurdity and self-contradiction!

But what did he mean when he said, We are not of them who draw back unto perdition? &c. Answer: we are not AT PRESENT of that number.—It has been observed already on chap. x. verse 25. that many of the converted Hebrews had forsaken the assembling of themselves together, and that there was danger the rest would follow their example. Now as this epistle was written on purpose to prevent this evil, the apostle, both in the passage under consideration, as well as elsewhere, lays before them the dreadful state of apostates. But that this might not discourage them, and cause them to abandon themselves to despair, he very judiciously tells them, that whatever *danger* they were in of becoming apostates, they were not, AT PRESENT, of that number; but rather of the number of those who *yet* believed to the saving of the soul.

I therefore conclude, notwithstanding all that has been said to the contrary, that the evil which the apostle here supposed the Hebrews to be in danger of was, so to neglect

lect this salvation as to draw back unto TOTAL and FINAL APOSTASY.

15. Another proof that falling away was the evil the apostle apprehended the Hebrews to be in danger of is, chap. xii. verse 3. "For consider him that ENDURED such contradiction of sinners against himself, lest ye be WEARIED and FAINT in your mind." Καμνειν, literally signifies, To be tired. The expression is agonistical, and belongs to those who are worsted, or overcome in fight, and who give over the combat through despair of success. So Dr. *Hammond* tells us from *Phavorinus*, that it signifies, "To give over to despair—to play the "coward or run-away." He also tells us that ψυχαις εκλυεσθαι signifies, "To turn "coward or pusillanimous, such as whose "souls within them fall away like water, "dissolve; and it is spoken of those who "give over the attempt as hopeless, fly "disheartened, or crest-fallen, out of the "field*." The continuators of *Pool* expound

* See Hammond on the place, Notes *(b)* and *(c)*.

pound the place thus: "Left faintness, "languishing, or deficiency of soul, that is, "of vigour, strength, and activity of heart "should befal them, and so they should "LIE DOWN and CEASE to run the chris- tian race*." *Suicerus* says, Καμνειν, signifies to faint, and also to die, whence the depart ed are also called καμνοντες†.

Now this was really the case. These Hebrews had entered the list on their first receiving the gospel, and for a while had couragiously carried on the encounter, but when they saw that instead of drawing to an end, it was still growing heavier and heavier, they were so disheartened, as to think of yielding, and of giving up all for lost. And therefore to fortify them against this, the apostle lays before them the example of Christ, who not only *took up* the cross, but also ENDURED it, verse 2. that is, who not only exposed himself, for the present, or only for a short time, to the contradiction of sinners; but EN-
DURED

* Pool's Comment.   † Thes. Eccles.

DURED, *patiently* ENDURED it, to the end. Now, says the apostle, consider him, and learn from his example; so you shall not grow weary, but endure to the end, as he did before you.—Again, he tells them, verse 4. "Ye have not resisted, μεχρις αιματος, as far as blood, striving against sin." As if he had said, You ought not to be disheartened by your present sufferings; for you have not gone so far as the *Athletæ* of old did in the Olympic games, who did not give over after brandishing their weapons, nor after slight skirmishing; but went on to that part of the combat which was often attended with blood and death. Now your past and present conflicts, are only like their slight skirmishes; and as the prize which you contend for, is so much better than theirs, it would be very absurd for you to grow weary, and give up the encounter before you go so far as they did. It is therefore certain, from what has been said, that FALLING AWAY was the evil which the apostle intended by, growing weary and faint in their minds.

16. The

16. The next proof of the point we have in the 12th and 13th verses of this chapter. "Wherefore lift up the hands which hang down, and the feeble knees: and make straight paths for your feet, left that which is lame be TURNED OUT OF THE WAY; but let it rather be healed." From these words it is certain, that TURNING OUT OF THE WAY was the evil which the apostle apprehended these Hebrews to be in danger of.—Now the question is, What he meant by turning out of the way? The greek word, εκτραπῃ, may be taken either for spraining a joint or sinew, by which means walking is rendered impracticable: or else it may be taken for turning out of, and leaving the right way. The former of these significations agrees best with the metaphors of lameness and healing, which are mentioned presently after, but the other agrees best with the preceding words concerning making straight paths for the feet, left that which is lame ALREADY be turned out of the way.—To understand the words in the former sense, would be to make nonsense of the passage; for it would

suppose

suppose the apostle to say, Make straight paths for your feet, lest that which is sprained already be sprained! lest that which is lame already be made lame! lest that which already halteth be made to halt! But if we take the words in the other sense, the meaning is easy, clear, and regular. Make straight paths for your feet—Remove, so far as in you lies, every impediment and difficulty out of the path, or way of duty, lest that which is lame—the tempted, the feeble, the halting soul, who has not courage enough to surmount many and great difficulties, be turned out of the way which leads to heaven.—And to this agrees Dr. *Doddridge*'s paraphrase: " Make straight
" paths for your feet. Regulate matters
" so, that the way of duty may be as ob-
" vious and easy as possible, that the in-
" firm, the lame, and the decrepit, may
" not, by discouragements and temptations,
" be turned out of the way, or thrown
" down; but that every such feeble tra-
" veller in the way to Zion, may rather
" be healed; recovered from falls or weak-
" ness, and strengthened to a course of
" more

"more strenuous and PERSEVERING pi-
"ety*." *Diodati* expounds it thus: "Make
"straight—make the way of the gospel
"plain and easy for you, by your volun-
"tary obedience, and using it—lest those
"who have neglected to strengthen them-
"selves in christian virtues be, through
"GOD's just punishment, put out of the
"way into APOSTASY‡." The continuators of *Pool* expound it thus: "Lest being
"lame, or halting in their minds between
"Judaism and Christianity, because of the
"violent persecution of them by their in-
"fidel brethren, they should be TURNED
"ASIDE OUT OF GOD's WAYS, erring and
"deviating from the truth of the gospel,
"but rather that they be restored to it, so
"as no sufferings upon that account, under
"GOD's hand, might make them suppress
"the truth, or expose them to APOSTA-
"SY∥." *Jacobus Capellus* observes that the
original word, εκτραπη, means, "*plane per-*
"*vertatur ac penitus immutetur*," should be
ALTO-

* See Doddridge on the place. ‡ Diodati on the place. ∥ Pool's Comment.

ALTOGETHER PERVERTED, and TOTALLY ALTERED: τρεπειν, adds he, "*est mutare,*" to turn, "εκτρεπειν, *prorsus immutare,*" to ALTER ENTIRELY ||. From all that has been said, I conclude, that apostasy from Christ and his gospel was what the apostle meant by turning, or being turned out of the way.

17. Another passage which shews that falling away was the evil intended, is the 15th verse of this chapter. "Looking diligently, lest any man fail of the grace of GOD, lest any root of bitterness springing up trouble you, and thereby many be defiled."—By the grace of GOD is meant, 1. His favour; and 2. Those inward privileges, of light, power, &c. which are bestowed on all who enjoy that favour. By failing of the grace of God, cannot be meant, to fail of *receiving* it; seeing, as I have demonstrated above, that these Hebrews had already received it. What therefore the apostle intended by the expression was,

|| Syn. Crit. in loc.

was, failing to RETAIN the grace of GOD, or failing to PERSEVERE. Hence the words in the original, υϛερων απο, are frequently rendered, FALL FROM the grace of GOD, and so our translators have rendered them in the margin. And that this is the true import of the expressions, we learn farther from Deut. xxix. verse 18. from whence the apostle quoted them. " Lest there be among you any man or woman, or family, or tribe, whose *heart* TURNETH AWAY this day from the Lord our GOD, to go and serve the gods of these nations; lest there should be among you a root that beareth gall and wormwood." Now it is certain that the apostle quoted this passage to shew these Hebrews, that they were in danger of the same kind of evil which their predecessors were in danger of in the days of Moses and the prophets. But that was the evil of APOSTASY, or turning away from the Lord their GOD. Therefore it was APOSTASY, or turning away from the Lord our GOD, that the apostle intended in this passage.

And

And so evident is the truth of this, that Calvinists and Arminians equally agree in asserting it. Dr. *Hammond* expounds the place, " Taking all care that ye walk like " Christians, THAT YE FALL NOT OFF " from the gospel state*." Dr. *Whitby* tells us, that " υσερηκεναι, is the same with " αφισασθαι, to depart from the grace of " God, which bringeth salvation, or, to " depart from the faith, and, by so doing, " fall short of the promised rest, Heb. iv. " 1. The words of the apostle, and his " *scope*, which is to prevent the Jews from " BACKSLIDING from Christianity to Ju‑ " daism, and the following exhortation, " not to refuse him that speaketh now, ver. " 25. and εχειν την χαριν, TO RETAIN AND " HOLD FAST the grace of GOD, verse 28. " sufficiently shew†." So Mr. *G. M.* in his learned and judicious comment, saith, " The author here alludes to the words of " Moses, Deut. xxix. 18. wherein he like‑ " wise speaketh of APOSTATES. By roots of
bitter‑

---

* Hammond on the place   † Whitby on the place.

"bitterness—he understands APOSTATES‖." Mr. *Trapp*'s observation is, "Perseverance crowns all*;" from whence it is evident that he understood the passage as speaking of perseverance. Dr. *Doddridge*'s paraphrase is, "Look to it therefore, with the the greatest attention and care, for yourselves and one another, lest any one, BY APOSTASY from the christian religion, fall short of the grace of GOD‡." In "King *Edward* the Sixth's Bible it is, "Take heed that no man FALL AWAY *from the* GRACE of God;" and on these words, left any root of bitterness springing up trouble you," &c. the Note is, "Of heresies, or APOSTASY§." The continuators of *Pool* render it, fail of, or "FALL FROM" *the* GRACE of GOD✢. *Beza* hath it, "Take heed that no man FALL FROM," &c. and on those words, left any root of bitterness, &c. the Note is, "That no heresy or BACKLSLIDING be an offence†." "Dr. *Heylin* saith, "Superintend what passes

---

‖ See on the place. * Trapp's Comment on the place. ‡ Dr. Doddridge on the place. § King Edward's Bible on the place. ✢ Pool's Comment. † Beza in loc.

"paffes among you, left any one fhould
"FALL AWAY FROM GRACE†." The
Dutch Annotators expound it, "Looking
"to it left any one ftay behind [that is,
"abide behind, TURN AWAY] from the
"grace of GOD§." Mr. *Henry* faith,
"Here the apoftle enters a ferious caveat
"againft APOSTASY, and backs it with
"an awful example‡." It is therefore cer
tain that falling away, or apoftafy, was the
evil fpoken of in this place.

18. The next proof of the propofition
we have in verfe 25. of the fame chapter.
" See that ye refufe not him that fpeaketh: for if they efcaped not, who refufed
him that fpake on earth, much more fhall
not we efcape, if WE TURN FROM HIM,
αποςρεφομενοι, or turning away from him
that fpeaketh from heaven. The evil here
fpoken of is, TURNING AWAY from him
that fpeaketh from heaven; that is, from
Chrift. But the queftion is, What is meant

L

by

---

† Heylin on the place. § Dutch Annot. on the
place. ‡ Henry on the place.

by turning away from him? It cannot mean, to turn away so as never to give him a hearing: seeing that these Hebrews had already heard him in this sense, as we learn from chap. ii. verse 1. yea, and believed in him also, to the saving of the soul, chap. x. verse 38. Therefore to turn away from him must signify, to discontinue their hearing of him: or, to refuse to PERSEVERE in hearing him.—This is evident from hence, that the turning away with which the apostle compared what he intended here, was of this sort. The Israelites of old had for some time hearkened to, and obeyed *Moses* when they were in Egypt; but when they were got through the Red Sea, into the wilderness, they turned away, they rebelled against him, and would not hearken unto him any longer: see Numb. xvi. Certain it is, then, that the turning away here spoken of by the apostle was that of APOSTASY. And concerning the antient Israelites, I would observe, that their turning away from him who spake on earth was TOTAL and FINAL; seeing they escaped

not,

not, as the apostle tells us; but died without mercy. It therefore follows, that the turning away from Christ, which the apostle compares with that turning away from him who spake on earth, is TOTAL and FINAL also.

19. The last evidence, of this sort, which I shall bring, we have, verses 28, 29. " Wherefore we receiving a kingdom which cannot be moved, let us have grace, whereby we may serve GOD acceptably, with reverence and godly fear. For our GOD is a consuming fire." The question here is, What are we to understand by *having* grace? The words in the original, are, Εχωμεν χαριν, and are often rendered HOLD FAST grace; and it is thus that our English translators have rendered them in the margin. " It is the observation of " critics here and elsewhere, says Dr. *Whit-* " *by*, that εχειν, to have, is often put for " κατεχειν, TO RETAIN and HOLD FAST: so " εχειν πιστιν και αγαθην συνειδησιν, is to HOLD " FAST faith, and a good conscience, 1 Tim. " 1. 19. εχειν το μυστηριον της πιστεως, to HOLD

" the myſtery of faith; ὑποτυπωσιν ἐχειν, to
" HOLD FAST the form of ſound words,
" 2 Tim. 1. 13." And that the words muſt
be rendered thus, in the paſſage under conſideration, is evident. For as theſe Hebrews were Chriſtian believers at the time
the apoſtle wrote to them, they muſt be
ſuppoſed to be in poſſeſſion of grace: of
conſequence, if, by having grace, the apoſtle meant, let us endeavour to get poſſeſſion of it; this would be to ſay, Let us
labour to get that which we have already!
But, on the other hand, if we ſuppoſe them,
firſt, to be in poſſeſſion of grace, and, ſecondly, to be in danger of loſing it, the
apoſtle's exhortation, to hold it faſt, and not
to let it go on any conſideration, was very
neceſſary and proper. It is therefore evident, that when the apoſtle ſaid, let us
have grace, his meaning was, let us hold
it faſt, and, by ſo doing, continue to have
it. Accordingly the learned *Diodati* expounds it, " Let us—KEEP ourſelves in
" the fruition of GOD's grace, and of the
gift

"gift of his Spirit*." Mr. G. M. in his very judicious comment on the place faith, "*Have* is here put for RETAIN or HOLD." And Professor *Dickson* hath it, "Let us "*have* grace, or HOLD FAST THE GRIP of "GRACE‖."—" Let us HOLD FAST GRACE," said the Continuators of *Pool*‡.—said the Assembly of Divines†:—said *Sam. Clark*§. *Grotius* and *Piscator* say, " εχωμεν, pro κατεχωμεν," *let us have*, for LET US RETAIN‡. " εχειν, pro κρατειν," says *Beza*, *to have*, for TO HOLD FAST**. So that the meaning of those expressions (to use the words of *Beza*, *Estius*, and *Jacobus Capellus*) is, "*Firmiter* "*retineamus, nec ullis tentationibus ab ea* "*nos sinamus revelli:*" Let us firmly RETAIN GRACE, nor let us suffer it to be TORN FROM US by any temptations††— Agreeable to all this, the Dutch Annotators render it, " Let us hold (fast) grace [name- " ly, which we have already received↩."

Again,

* See *Diodati* on the place. ‖ *Dickson* on the place. ‡ *Pool's* Comment. † Assembly's Annotations. § *Clark's* Comment ‡ *Grotius et Piscator in loc* ** *Beza in loc.* †† *Syn. Crit in loc.* ↩ *Dutch Annot.* on the place.

Again, that the apostle here supposed the Hebrews to be in danger of TOTAL and FINAL apostasy is evident from the following words, For our GOD is, Πυρ καταναλισκον, a consuming fire. This indeed his very name imports. So *Gregory Nazianzen*, Απο τε αιθειν ετυμολογηται, δια το δαπαντικον των μοχθηρων εξεων, και γαρ πῦρ καταναλισκον εντευθεν λεγεται. It (the word Θεος) is derived from αιθειν, to consume; on account of his power of consuming vicious affections*. So *Damascenus*: Το Θεος ονομα λεγεται εκ τε αιθειν, ο εστι καιειν· ο γαρ Θεος πυρ καταναλισκον πασαν κακιαν εστι· "The name, GOD, is taken from αιθειν, which is, to burn; for GOD is a fire, consuming all wickedness‡." And these words are added by the apostle, as a reason to enforce the performance of the aforesaid duties; as if he had said, Hold fast the grace you have, that therewith, or thereby, you may serve GOD in a manner which shall be acceptable unto him. For if you do not, you shall experience him to be

---

* Greg Nazianzen. Orat. 36. fol. 589.   ‡ Damasc. Orthod. Fidei, lib. cap. 12.

be a confuming fire, in caufing his fiery indignation to devour you, chap. x. verfe 27. or as the Dutch Annotators have it, " As a confuming fire towards them that " are difobedient or APOSTATES*." It is therefore certain from the nature of the punifhment which is here threatened (which none but thofe who apoftatize TOTALLY and FINALLY, are capable of) that the apoftle here intended TOTAL and FINAL APOSTASY.

But it may be objected, that " In the " xiiith chap. and 5th verfe, GOD hath " faid, I will never leave thee nor forfake " thee. In which words, according to the " original, there are five negatives, Ου μη " σε ανω, ουδ' ου μη σε εγκαταλιπω· that is, I " will not leave thee, neither will I not " not forfake thee: or thus; I will not, " I will not leave thee, I will never, never, " never forfake thee." To this I anfwer, that the number of negatives, fuppofe they were five hundred, or five thoufand, does not in the leaft degree *fhew* the *fenfe* of the place:

* Dutch Annot. on the place.

place: the very most that they can do is, to shew that whatever the sense is, it is emphatical: and therefore, let any one declaim as he will on his five negatives, it is infallibly sure, that nothing more than this can be inferred from them.

But what is the meaning of the words, I will never leave thee, nor forsake thee? I answer, it is impossible for them to mean, I will not, leave it in thy power to neglect this salvation; I will not, no I will not suffer thee to let it slip. I will never, never, never suffer thee to let go thy confidence or the rejoicing of the hope; to harden thy heart as in the provocation; to have an evil heart of unbelief in departing from the living GOD; to be hardened through the deceitfulness of sin; to fall so as to be incapable of being renewed again unto repentance; to fall by unbelief, after the example of the Israelites of old; to cast away thy confidence which hath great recompence of reward; to draw back unto perdition; to be wearied and faint in thy mind; to fall from the grace of GOD; or to let it depart in such manner, as to know by experience that he is a confuming fire. I fay, it is impoffible for the meaning to be, I will not, I will not fo leave thee, I will never, never, never fo forfake thee, as to render it poffible for thee to fall into thofe evils which I have fo often declared thou art in danger of, and which I have fo often warned thee againft.

But what then do they mean? That God would not fail to provide for his people while they were obedient to, and trufted in him.—As this promife was originally made to *Joshua*, and afterwards unto thefe Hebrews, it refpected temporal things and thefe only. As it was made to *Joshua* it only refpected his conqueft of Canaan. So we read, Joſh. i. 1.—"The Lord fpake unto *Joshua* faying, verfe 2. *Moses* my fervant is dead; now therefore arife, go over this Jordan, thou, and all this people, unto the land which I do give unto them, even to the children of Ifrael. verfe 3. Every place that the fole of your foot fhall tread upon, that have I given unto you.—Verfe 4. From the wildernefs and this Lebanon,

even

even unto the great river Euphrates—verse 5. There shall not be a man able to stand before thee all the days of thy life. as I was with *Moses*, so I will be with thee. I will not fail thee nor forsake thee." It is therefore evident that here is nothing promised but temporal success.

And that this promise was conditional is clear beyond a doubt. For when the people fell into disobedience, their enemies were so far from being unable to stand before them, that they were not able to stand before their enemies. So we read, chap. 7. verse 5. " And the men of *Ai* smote of them about thirty and six men : for they chased them from before the gate, even unto Shebazim, and smote them in the going down: wherefore the hearts of the people melted and became as water." Verse 11. God informs *Joshua* of the cause of this disaster. " Israel hath sinned, and they have transgressed my covenant which I commanded." Verse 12. " Therefore the children of Israel could not stand before their enemies, but turned their backs before

before their enemies, becaufe they were accurfed :" it is then added, " neither will I BE WITH YOU ANY MORE, except ye deftroy the accurfed from among you."

From all that hath been faid, obferve, firft, that although GOD hath faid, " There fhall not a man be able to ftand before thee all the days of thy life," yet when they difobeyed him, there were men, even the men of Ai, who not only ftood before them, but deftroyed fome of them, and chafed the reft quite away. Obferve, fecondly, that although God had faid, " I will not fail thee, nor forfake thee;" yet we find that when they had finned, he NOT ONLY FORSOOK THEM; but alfo declared, " Neither WILL I BE WITH YOU ANY MORE except ye deftroy the accurfed from amongft you." It is therefore certain that this promife, as originally made, was only a CONDITIONAL promife of fuccefs in conquering and poffeffing the land of Canaan.

As it is applied to the converted Hebrews, it is a promife of outward provifions. This is evident from the context.
" Let

" Let your converfation be without cove-toufnefs, and be content with fuch things as ye have: for he hath faid, I will never leave thee, nor forfake thee."—For a better underftanding of thefe words, let it be obferved, that the converted Hebrews had formerly been fpoiled and plundered in their worldly goods, on account of their attachment to the Gofpel. This, for a while, they took joyfully. But when they looked forward, and faw nothing in this world but profpects of greater poverty and diftrefs, many of them were in danger of too great folicitude about thefe worldly things: and it is not improbable that fome of them were in danger of leaving Chrift, becaufe his religion expofed them to great poverty, as well as to other worldly inconveniencies.

To prevent this, the apoftle very feafonably faid, Let your τροπος, your difpofition, your manner, your turnings and windings for a livelihood, be without covetoufnefs; that is, without anxious, miftruftful care; and be content with fuch things as ye have,

have, or, as it is often rendered, with the present things: for he hath said, "I will never leave thee, nor forsake thee." It is therefore certain, that neither the text nor context do, in the smallest degree, authorize us to expound this promise otherwise than as speaking of temporal things. And, that even in this sense, it must be understood conditionally, appears from hence, that when GOD made it to *Joshua*, it was certainly conditional; for though the condition was not mentioned in the promise, the event fully shews it to be conditional, as I have shewn above. And as we have no authority to understand the same promise conditionally in the days of *Joshua*, and unconditionally in the days of *Paul*, I conclude that it must be understood conditionally in this epistle to the Hebrews: and that, upon the whole, the meaning is, I will not, I will not leave thee to want the necessaries of life, while thou trustest in me, I will never, never, never forsake thee, while thou art obedient to my word. *Estius*, after observing that the original promise was made to *Joshua*, says, " *Extenditur*
"ad

"*ad omnes justos, et ad omnem temporalem necessitatem*"—it extends to all the righteous, and to every TEMPORAL necessity[*]. *Junius* confines it yet more when he says, "*Pertinet ad pios omnes vocationi suæ hærentes:*" it belongs to all the righteous, WHO ADHERE TO THEIR VOCATION[†]. This passage, therefore, does in no wise militate against the general conclusion maintained in this discourse.

Having demonstrated from nineteen texts in this epistle, that the evil which the apostle apprehended these Hebrews to be in danger of, was total and final apostasy; and having considered the three texts (which are all that can be found in the epistle) which have the appearance of an objection to the general conclusion; I shall sum up all that hath been said on this head, by giving a brief account of the OCCASION and DESIGN of the epistle, and of the apostle's manner of reasoning therein.

The Christian religion being so contrary to the corrupt principles and practice of the world,

---

[*] Estius in loc.   [†] Junius in loc.

world, thofe who embraced and propagated it were, on thofe accounts, rendered very odious wherever they came. The confequence of this was, that heavy perfecutions were raifed againft them in moft places. The converted Hebrews, becaufe they had turned their back on the law of Mofes, and embraced the religion of that Jesus whom their rulers had crucified, were exceedingly perfecuted by their countrymen. Sometimes the unconverted Hebrews perfecuted their converted brethren themfelves; at other times they ftirred up the Heathen, who were round about, to do it. By thefe means the believing Hebrews had a great fight of afflictions, chap. x. verfe 32. and were made gazing-ftocks, both by reproaches and afflictions, verfe 33. and experienced the fpoiling of their goods, which for a while they took joyfully, verfe 34.

But this was not all: for as the Chriftian religion was then a new thing in the world, it is natural to fuppofe that the new converts had many fcruples, and reafonings in themfelves concerning the lawfulnefs of what they had done in embracing it. And what added to these scruples was, the constant endeavour of the judaizing teachers to lay stumbling-blocks in the way of these Hebrews, which they too often effected by means of their divers and strange doctrines, mentioned chap. xiii. verse 9. The consequence of this opposition, both from within and without, was, that great numbers of the Hebrews apostatized from Christ and his gospel, and went back to the law of Moses, while the fluctuating state of the rest, gave the apostles too much reason to fear a general, if not an universal apostasy. Now this apparent danger was the occasion of this epistle, and the DESIGN of it was, to prevent the threatened evil if possible.

And that I am not alone in this opinion, the following testimonies abundantly declare. *Clemens Alexandrinus* saith, Επει και Παυλος τοις Εβραιοις γραφων τοις επαναλαμπτουσιν εις νομον εκπισεως, that is, Paul also writing to the Hebrews, RELAPSING from the faith unto the Law, saith ||, &c. Now if the other Fathers

---
|| Strom. lib. vi. fol. 645. Colon. edit.

Fathers, so often quoted in the preceding pages, such as *Ignatius, Chrysostom, Oecumenius, Ambrose, Cyprian, Phavorinus, Theophylact, Greg. Nazianzen, Damascenus,* &c. expounded the particular passages above cited, according to their view of the scope of the whole epistle (which would be absurd to suppose they did not) they must be supposed to agree with *Clemens Alexandrinus*, that it was intended as a CAVEAT AGAINST APOSTASY. And the same must be said of those of later date, which I have so often cited: such as *Grotius, Erasmus, Camero, Ribera, Calvin, Junius, Gomarus, Gerhardus, Capellus, Menochius, Aretius, Piscator, Suicerus, Beza,* &c. For we cannot suppose that such profound Commentators and Critics would give one uniform exposition of so many particular passages, in this, or any other epistle, which they thought was unconnected with the occasion and design of the whole.

To what has been said, I shall add the express testimony of a great number of other writers, many of whom are of a more modern date.

The learned *Marlorat* says, "*Utrâque parte se epistolæ eos hortatur; illic ne Christum rejiciant, hic autem ut Christo fidant, et per patientiam in veritate persistant:*" that is, In both parts of the epistle, he (the apostle) earnestly exhorts them, on the one hand, that they would not *reject Christ*; but wholly trust in Him by Faith, and PATIENTLY PERSEVERE in the Truth†. So *Ostervald*, "*Il exhorte les Hebreux a la perseverance dans la foi:*" He exhorts the Hebrews to PERSEVERANCE in the Faith*. *Le Clerc* says, "*Ut animus Christianis addatur, quo constantes ac perseverantes sint,*" &c. the apostle wrote this epistle, To animate the Christians, that they might be CONSTANT and PERSEVERING in the Faith§. The great *Bengelius* says, "*Totus in id incumbit, ut fratrum fidem in Jesum Christum confirmet:*" that is, The apostle employs ALL HIS STRENGTH ON THIS SINGLE POINT, that he might CONFIRM the faith of the brethren in our Lord Jesus Christ‖. So
Michaelis

† See Comment. page 966. * Ostervald in loc.
§ Le Clerc's preface on the place. ‖ See his preface to this Epistle.

Michaelis, 'He (the apostle) writes this "epistle—to the Christians in Palestine. "A severe persecution, not only deprived "them of the apostle *James*; but rendered "almost the whole church WAVERING in "the faith ||." The learned *Hallett* says, "The Christians were continually persecut- "ed by the unbelieving Jews—Heb. x. "32—36. chap. xii. 4, 5. By these per- "secutions they were tempted to APOSTA- "TISE from Christianity*." Dr. *Roberts* in his *Clavis Bibliorum* saith, "The apos- "tle's SCOPE IS—To exhort the Hebrews "to CONSTANCY in the Faith—from the "peril of APOSTASY §." Again he saith, "The apostle exhorts the Hebrews faithfully "to hearken to and obey Christ's doctrine, "and constantly to PERSEVERE in the Faith "of the Gospel; and that against all "grounds and occasions of APOSTASY ‡." *Calmet* saith, The apostle "addresses him- "self to the BELIEVERS in Palestine, to "CONFIRM them against those evils which "they

---

|| See Lectures, page 360. * Hallet's Synop. as quoted by Dr. Lardner in his history of the Apostles, page 383. § See page 542. ‡ Ibid. 543.

" they were about to suffer from the unbe-
" lieving Jews†." *Cradock*, in his apostolic
History says, St. *Paul* " exhorts them—to
" be STEDFAST in the Faith : representing
" to them the horrible danger of RELAPS-
" ING, after they had tasted of the gift of
" the Spirit‡." Mr. *G. M.* whose comment
is so strongly recommended by Mr. *J.
Downham*, saith, " The principal end of
" it [this epistle] is to exhort to CONSTAN-
" CY and PERSISTANCE in the Christian
" religion§." The learned Dr. *Sykes*, in
his paraphrase and notes saith, " It was—
" wrote to Hebrew-Christians—to keep
" them steady to their professions, and to
" guard them from RELAPSING into Juda-
" ism*." Dr. *Lightfoot* saith, that The apostle's " intention is, if he can, to argue them
" into an establishment against that griev-
" ous APOSTASY that was then on foot‖."
Dr. *Hammond*, saith, that The Hebrews—
" began to forsake the Christian assemblies,
" and to fall off from the profession of their
" faith :

---

† Calmet's Dictionary, page 529.   ‡ See page 301.
§ See the Argument to his Comment & Introduc-
tion.   ‖ Harmony of the N. Testament, page 141.

" faith: which being" (observe it well)—
" THE OCCASION of this monitory epistle,
" THE SUBJECT consequently is, to con-
" firm them in the truth," and " to repre-
" sent the great danger and sin of FALLING
" OFF*." Dr. *Whitby* saith, that this epistle was " written to persons now relapsing
" from Christ to Moses†." Again, in his
discourse on the Five Points, he saith,
" Now to *prevent this apostasy* of the be-
" lieving Jews the epistle to the Hebrews
" was manifestly written: and as the ex-
" cellent Dr. *Barrow* used to say, that it was
" written" (observe well.) " AGAINST
" THE DOCTRINE OF PERSEVERANCE‡."
In the Argument to the epistle to the Hebrews, in *Edward* the Sixth's Bible, we
have these words, " Wherefore according
" to the example of the old fathers we must
" CONSTANTLY believe in him, that being
" sanctified by his justice, taught by his
" wisdom, and governed by his power,
" we may stedfastly and couragiously, even
" to

* Preface to this Epistle.   † Preface to this Epistle.
‡ See Discourse on the Five Points, page 414.

" to the end, continue or persevere in hope
" of that joy that is set before us*." Dr.
Owen, the great champion of the Calvinists in the last century, in his learned exposition on the epistle to the Hebrews, saith, St. *Paul* " had a SPECIAL eye unto the
" APOSTASY of some of the Hebrews, oc-
" casioned by the persecutions which then
" began to grow high against them. What-
" ever argument or testimony in his passage
" gave him advantage to press an exhorta-
" tion unto CONSTANCY, and to deter them
" from BACKSLIDING, he lays hold upon
" it†." Again, says the same author,
" As it is likely from this epistle, many of
" them who had made profession of the
" gospel, rather than they would utterly
" forego their old way of worship, DE-
" SERTED THE FAITH, and cleaving to
" their unbelieving countrymen, PERISH-
" ED IN THEIR APOSTASY, whom our
" apostle in an especial manner forewarns
" of their INEVITABLE DESTRUCTION, by
" the fire of God's indignation‡." Again,
" All

---

* King Edward's Bible. † Dr. Owen's Exposition, page 38. ‡ Ibid. page 43.

"All the fears the apostle had of their "APOSTASY into Judaism—arose from their "adherence unto, and zeal for the law of "Moses*." Again, "HIS PRINCIPAL "END THEREFORE IN THIS WHOLE EPIS-"TLE (AS HATH BEEN DECLARED) was "to prevail with the Hebrews unto STED-"FASTNESS *in the faith of the Gospel* §." *Echard* saith that "These Hebrew—con-"verts" had "heavy persecutions both "from Jews and Gentiles—besides a train "of plausible insinuations to reduce them "to their antient Mosaic institutions, to "which many of them had turned of late, "APOSTATISING from the purity of the "Christian faith. Wherefore, partly to "warn and instruct them, and partly to "encourage and support them, he [*Paul*] "wrote this celebrated epistle†." The Assembly of Divines in their Argument to this epistle say, "The apostle observing, "that the Hebrews (at least a great part "of them) were ready to FALL FROM THE
"FAITH

---

* Ibid. page 353.   § Ibid.   † Ecclesiastical History, page 229.

"FAITH OF CHRIST into their former Ju-
"daism, by reason of the cruel persecu-
"tions which they suffered, HENCE TOOK
"OCCASION TO WRITE THIS EPISTLE
"UNTO THEM; wherein he laboureth to
"CONFIRM them in THAT FAITH which
"THEY HAD RECEIVED, and to stir them
"up to stand STEDFAST IN IT; and that
"by divers arguments: as first, from the
"excellency of Christ's nature," &c. "Se-
"condly from the DANGER OF APOSTA-
"SY‡." Mr. *Sam. Clark* saith, "The
"Scope of it is this: the BELIEVING, or
"CHRISTIAN Hebrews suffered under two
"great evils, one inward, the other out-
"ward; the former was a great error, in
"joining Christ and Moses—the latter was
"their grievous persecution from their
"countrymen for *turning Christians*, where-
"upon many of THEM were in GREAT
"DANGER OF APOSTASY" — "Against
"the latter, their persecution, he endea-
"vours to fortify them by laying down
"*several motives* to, and *grounds of* PERSE-
"VERANCE

‡ Assembly's Annotations.

VERANCE *in the* FAITH *and* TRUTH||." Bishop *Fell*, in his introduction to this epistle saith,—" Some of them" (the converted Hebrews) " began to use great complian-
" ces and *weariness in their religion, and to*
" FORSAKE *the Christian assemblies*. See He-
" brews x. 25. and some others to RE-
" LAPSE and FALL AWAY FROM THE
" CHRISTIAN FAITH. He (the apostle)
" represents to them the great sin, and des-
" perate condition of APOSTASY, and the
" fruitlessness of former endeavours and
" suffering, without PERSEVERANCE∗."
Mr. *Henry* saith, " The DESIGN of this
" epistle was to promote and press the BE-
" LIEVING Hebrews to a constant adhe-
" rence to the Christian faith, and PERSE-
" VERANCE in it§." Dr. *Gill* says, " The
" OCCASION and DESIGN of it is,"—" to
" exhort them to PERSEVERANCE, and to
" strengthen them against APOSTASY†."
Dr. *Doddridge* saith, " Now the MANIFEST

N   DESIGN

|| Clark's Comment.   ∗ Fell on the Hebrews.
§ Argument to the epistle to the Heb.   † Ecclesiastical History.

" DESIGN of St. Paul in this epistle is,
" To CONFIRM the Jewish Christians in the
" faith and practice of the gospel of Christ,
" which they might be in danger of DESRT-
" ING, either through the insinuation, or
" ill treatment of their persecutors§." The
great calvinian *Diodati* saith, the " Hebrews
" to whom it" (this epistle) " was direct-
" ed, were Jews CONVERTED to Christ."
and that the apostle shews " them the
" DANGER OF FALLING INTO APOSTASY to
" the IRREVOCABLE DAMNATION OF
" THEIR SOULS‖." The calvinian author
of Critica Sacra saith, " The apostle writes
" to the Hebrews not to FALL AWAY from
" Christianity to Judaism, " which," saith
he, " is the FULL SCOPE OF THIS EPIS
" TLE*." Mr. *Collyer*, in his Sacred Interpreter, gives the following account a little more at large. " By the Hebrews are
" —meant—those of the Jewish people
" WHO HAD RECEIVED THE FAITH.—Ma-
" ny of these were in danger of FALLING
" AWAY

---

§ Preface to this epistle. ‖ Diodati's Preface to this epistle. * See Leigh's Annotations.

" AWAY.—Now this being the cafe, the
" apoftle labours, the better to keep them
" fteady in their Chriftian profeffion—he
" fets forth the excellency of Chrift, as to
" his nature; he being the Son of God, and
" far above angels—and more excellent
" than Moles. Farther—the apoftle fhews
" the excellency of Chrift's priefthood—
" Then, as to facrifices—that the facrifice
" of himfelf which Chrift offered—was
" more effectual by far, than all the obla-
" tions and facrifices appointed by the law
" of Mofes—and therefore they [the He-
" brews] ought to KEEP STEDFAST TO
" THEIR CHRISTIAN profeffion, otherwife
" the danger would be great, even of their
" UTTER DESTRUCTION.

" This dangerous effect of APOSTASY the
" apoftle twice mentions. Firft in chap. vi.
" 4, 5, 6. where he tells them it would be
" impoffible to renew them again unto re-
" pentance, if after being enlightened with
" the knowledge of Chrift—and—endued
" with the divine Spirit—they fhould now
" CAST OFF their holy religion, and fo
" be-

"become APOSTATES FROM CHRISTIANI-
"TY, and fall back to Judaism.

"The like dangerous effect of APOSTA-
"SY the apostle repeats chap. x. 26, &c
"assuring them, there remaineth no more
"sacrifice for sin, but a certain fearful
"looking for of judgment—therefore he
"exhorts them to PERSEVERANCE. He
[the author] then observes, that "What
"has hitherto been mentioned is the SUB-
"STANCE of the epistle, to the beginning
"of the 11th chapter. He [the apostle]
"goes on chap. xi. to set before them the
"power of the grace of faith, and proposes
"the example of the saints in former times,
"and then tells them, chap. xii.—that all
"these examples of faith and CONSTANCY
"ought to be encouragements to them, to
"run with patience in the Christian race.
"Afterwards—he instructs them to adorn
"their christian profession—and (which was
"all along the MAIN DESIGN) to take heed
"that no one amongst them—should de-
"spise and CAST OFF their glorious privi-
"lege in Christ Jesus, and their interest in
"the gospel, and in being members of
Christ's

"Chrift's holy church, with the benefits
of the new covenant through Chrift's
blood.

"Laftly, chap. xiii. 1. &c. he gives
them fundry particular directions for a
chriftian life and behaviour, and then
again encourages them to PERSEVERE in
the chriftian faith§."

That this account is true, will fully appear from a more particular furvey of the contents of the whole epiftle.

Chap. i. The apoftle fhews that all former difpenfations were delivered to the world by men and angels, who were only fervants in what they did; but that the gofpel falvation was delivered by Chrift, who is the Son of God, and the Heir of all things. How naturally does he then infer the fuperiority of the Gofpel over the Law; and, of confequence, the great abfurdity of leaving the former for the fake of the latter!

Chap. ii. He obviates an objection which might be made to the fuperior exellency of Chrift,

---

§ See Sacred Interpreter, from page 275, 279.

Chrift, on account of his humiliation. To this end he shews that this humiliation was voluntary: that it was intended for many important purposes, viz. That we might be sanctified, verse 11. That through his death we might be delivered from death, verse 14, 15. And that Chrift, by experiencing our infirmities in his own person, might become a faithful and a merciful High-prieft, verse 17, 18. The inference then is, That his taking our nature upon him, and dying therein, is no argument of his inferiority, either to the prophets or to the angels; and therefore it is no excufe for thofe who APOSTATISE from the gofpel for the fake of the law.

Chap. iii. Here *Chrift* is particularly compared with *Mofes*, and fhewn to be fuperior to him in feveral refpects. As, 1. *Chrift* is the great builder of that houfe, of which *Mofes* is only a fmall part, verfe 3, 4. 2. *Chrift* is as a Son in his own houfe; but *Mofes* was only as a fervant in his mafter's houfe, verfe 5. Therefore *Chrift* and his falvation are fuperior to *Mofes* and his law, and ought not to be neglected on account of that which is inferior to it.—From verse 7. of this chapter, to verse 14. of the 4. chapter, the apostle shews the great danger of APOSTATISING from Christ, by the severe sentence which was passed on those who rebelled against *Moses,* and apostatised from his law.

Chap. v. *Christ* is compared to *Aaron,* and preferred to him on several accounts. As, 1. *Aaron* offered for his own, as well as for the sins of the people; but *Christ* offered only for the sins of others, having none of his own to offer for, verse 3. 2. *Christ* was not a priest after the order of *Aaron,* but after the order of *Melchisedec,* which was a superior order, verse 10.

Concerning *Melchisedec* and *Christ,* the apostle observed, that, through the dullness of the *Hebrews,* there were some things which they could not easily understand, verse 11,—14. He therefore calls on them, chap. vi. to labour for a more perfect acquaintance therewith; withal promising them his farther assistance, ver. 1—3. The necessity of their doing this, of their thus going on unto perfection, he enforced by the following confideration, that if they did not go forward, they would be in danger of APOSTATISING in fuch manner as would be irrecoverable, verfe 7, 8. From thence to the end of the chapter, he encouraged them to patience and PERSEVERANCE, by the confideration of the love, oath, and faithfulnefs of GOD; and, alfo, by the example of their father *Abraham*.

Chap. vii. The apoftle refumes the parallel between *Melchifedec* and *Chrift*, and fhews that they agree in title and defcent, verfe 1—3. and then from inftances wherein the priefthood of *Melchifedec* was preferable to the priefthood of Aaron, he infers the fuperiority of *Chrift's* prieft-hood over that of *Aaron's*, verfe 4—17. From thence to the end of the chapter he fhews that the priefthood of *Aaron* was only fubfervient to the priefthood of *Chrift*, in which it was confummated and abolifhed; and, of confequence, that all thofe legal obligations were thereby abolifhed. How naturally then did the apoftle infer the abfurdity of APOSTATISING from the gofpel to the law, feeing they who did this, not only left the greater

for

for the lesser; but also left that which remained in full force, for the sake of that which was disannulled.

Chap. viii. is employed, partly in recapitulating what had been demonstrated before concerning the superior dignity of our great High-priest, verse 1—5 and partly in shewing the superior excellency of the new covenant as established in Christ, and as containing better promises; verse 6, to the end of the chapter. From this last consideration, the impropriety of going from the new covenant to the old, is as naturally inferred, as from any other of the afore mentioned considerations.

With the same view the apostle, chap. ix. compares *Christ* and his priesthood, to the tabernacle of old, and to what the high-priest did therein on the great day of atonement; in all things giving *Christ* the preference, from verse 1. to the end.

Chap. x. The apostle sets down the difference between the legal sacrifices and the sacrifice of *Christ*. The legal sacrifices were weak and could not put away sin, verse 1—4. but the sacrifice of *Christ* was powerful,

powerful, doing that which the other could not do, verse 5—10.

The next point of difference was between the legal priests who offered these sacrifices, and the High-priest of our profession. And, first, the legal priests were many, our's is one. Secondly, they stood when they presented their offerings to God; but *Christ* sits at the right hand of his Father. Thirdly, they offered often; but *Christ* once for all. Fourthly, they, with all their offerings could not put away the smallest sin; but *Christ*, by his one offering, put away all sin, verse 11—18. Now, from all these considerations, the apostle infers the great superiority of the Gospel over the Law, and consequently, the impropriety of leaving the former for the sake of the latter.

The next thing that the apostle does, is to improve his doctrine. This he does by shewing that, for the reasons above given, the Hebrews ought to cleave to *Christ*, to hold fast their profession, and not to forsake the assembling of themselves together. ver. 19—25. And as a farther inducement to cleave to *Christ*, and to PERSEVERE unto the end

end, he urges the consideration of the difficulties which they had overcome already; and also of the love which they had formerly shewn towards *Christ* and his gospel, verse 32—34. He also encouraged them not to cast away their confidence, seeing it had a great recompence of reward, which they should soon enjoy, if they PERSEVERED to the end, ver. 35—37. Another consideration which he urged was, that they ought not to depart from faith to the works of the law; because it is by faith that a just man liveth, and not by the works of the law; because God has no pleasure in those who draw back from faith in him; and because every one who does this, exposes himself to eternal perdition, verse 36—39.

Another inducement which he lay before them, to CONTINUE to expect salvation by faith and patience, was the consideration of the powerful effect of these graces, as exemplified in the patriarchs of old, and the rest of the ancient worthies: chapter the XI. throughout. " This chapter," according to Mr. *Perkins,* " depends on the " former, thus; we may read in the former
" chapter

" chapter, that many Jews having received
" the faith, and given their names to *Christ*,
" did afterwards FALL AWAY; therefore
" towards the end of the chapter, there
" is a notable exhortation tending to per-
" suade the Hebrews to PERSEVERE in
" faith unto the end."—" Now in this
" chapter he continues the same exhorta-
" tion: and the WHOLE CHAPTER (AS I
" TAKE IT) IS NOTHING ELSE in substance
" but one reason to urge the former exhor-
" tation to PERSEVERANCE in faith: and
" the reason is drawn from the excellency of
" it: for this chapter doth divers ways set
" down what an excellent GIFT of GOD
" FAITH IS: his WHOLE SCOPE therefore
" is manifest to be NOTHING ELSE, but to
" urge them to PERSEVERE and CONTINUE
" in THAT FAITH, proved at large to be so
" EXCELLENT a thing†."

And as a farther encouragement to patience and PERSEVERANCE he adds the example of *Christ*, chap. xii. verse 1—3. And
as to the afflictions they met with on the
gospel's

---

† See Perkin's Comment on the Epistle to the Hebrews, page 1.

gospel's account, he tells them that they ought not to be discouraged, and driven away from *Christ* on their account, seeing they were signs of the divine favour, and permitted to come upon them, only for their good, verse 4—11. He then exhorts them to encourage one another, to PERSEVERE in well-doing, verse 12—14. To watch over one another, lest any of them fall FROM THE GRACE OF GOD, verse 15—18. And seeing they were then in possession of privileges, gospel privileges, such as the law of *Moses* could not give, he exhorts them to HOLD FAST the grace they had, that thereby they might serve God, in such a manner as the great obligations they were under required; which alone would be acceptable unto him: and this they ought to do the rather, because if they did not, they would find God to be as much more severe to them, as his gospel is superior to the law, verse 19. to the end of the chapter.

Chap. xiii. He exhorts them, instead of APOSTATIZING, to CONTINUE their brotherly affection one for another, verse 1—3.

To CONTINUE their purity of behaviour; their dependance on GOD; and their regard for their teachers, verse 4—8. He exhorts them not to suffer themselves to be CARRIED ABOUT (from *Christ* and his gospel) by divers and strange doctrines, but rather to strive to be established in grace: which they would find to be of more service to them than running about after jewish ceremonies, verse 9. Again, he exhorts them to CLEAVE TO, and follow *Jesus* without the camp, and continually to give praise to GOD, through HIM, verse 9—16. and instead of TURNING AWAY after seducers, that they might avoid persecution, and the scandal of the cross, he exhorts them to submit to and obey their own Christian teachers, and to pray for their success and welfare, verse 17—19. concluding the whole with some salutations, and a solemn benediction, from verse 20. to the end.

Now if we closely attend to these general contents of the epistle, we shall find that EVERY ARGUMENT, and MODE OF REASONING, which would be *proper* in a treatise, wrote, professedly, on the sin and
dan-

danger of apostasy, is made use of in this epistle.

For, 1. As great temptations to prefer the law of *Moses* to the gospel of *Christ*, was one circumstance which exposed them to the danger of apostasy, nothing could be more to the purpose, than to shew them that the gospel is superior to the law. Now we have seen how largely this argument is prosecuted in chap. i. ii. iii. v. vii. viii. ix and x. If we reduce it to form, it runs as follows:

No one ought to prefer that which is less excellent unto that which is more so;

But the law is less excellent than the gospel:

Therefore none ought to prefer the law to the gospel, by apostatizing from the latter to the former.

2. Another argument, equally proper on such an occasion, is that taken from the consideration of the punishment which all apostates are exposed to. This argument is urged, chap. ii. verse 2, 3. chap. iii. verse 7. to the end. chap. iv. verse 1,—14. chap. vi. verse 4—8. chap. x. verse 26,—31.

31. chap. xii. verse 25, 28, 29. In most of these places the apostle compares the punishment which will be inflicted on apostates from Christ and his gospel, to that which was inflicted on the apostate Israelites of old. and he frequently shews that the former will be far greater than the latter. This argument is as follows,

You ought not to do that which will expose you to as great and greater punishment, than that which God inflicted on the rebellious Israelites of old;

But total and final apostasy from Christ will expose you to this;

Therefore you ought not totally and finally to apostatize from Christ.

3. Another argument proper on such an occasion, is that taken from the consideration of the great reward which God has promised to perseverance. This the apostle urges, chap. iii. verse 6. 14. chap. iv. verse 1, 9. chap v. verse 9. chap. vi. verse 9,—11. chap. ix. verse 28. chap. x. verse 35,—39. This argument runs thus:

You ought to be careful to do that which God has promised greatly to reward;

But

But he has promised you this on condition of your perseverance in the gospel of his Son;

Therefore you ought to be careful to persevere therein.

4. A fourth argument, which must operate powerfully on such an occasion, is taken from the consideration of losing their present privileges by apostatizing. This argument is insisted on, chap. ii. verse 11. to the end. chap. iii. verse 1. chap. iv. verse 3, 14,—16. chap. vi. verse 18,—20 chap. vii. verse 19. chap. viii. verse 10,—12. chap. ix. verse 14, 15. chap. x. verse 14,—22. chap xii. verse 22, 24, 28, chap. xiii. verse 10,—14. This argument runs thus:

You ought not to do that by which you will lose the gospel privileges you now enjoy.

But if you apostatize from Christ and his gospel, you will lose these.

Therefore you ought not to apostatize from *Christ* and his gospel.

5. A fifth argument very proper in such

a work is taken from the confideration of their former zeal and diligence, in cleaving to *Chrift,* and in profeffing his religion. This argument is handled, chap. vi. verfe 10. chap. x. verfe 32—34. The argument here is,

Thofe who have formerly been zealous in well-doing ought not to grow weary, but rather to be ftedfaft therein unto the end.

But you have formerly been zealous in your adherence to *Chrift,* and in profeffing his religion;

Therefore, you ought not to grow weary of adhering to *Chrift,* or of profeffing his religion.

6. Another argument proper on fuch an occafion is taken from the example of fuch perfons as are held in very high efteem. Now this argument is urged, chap. vi. verfe 12—15. chap. xi. throughout; chap. xii. verfe 1—3. Here the argument is,

Whatever you efteem as an excellency in the example of the holy men of old, you ought to imitate;

But you efteem as an excellency in their
example

example, that they were stedfast, and did not apostatize from God and his ways;

Therefore you ought to imitate their example in being stedfast, and in not apostatizing from *Christ* and his gospel.

From all that hath been said, in these several surveys of this epistle, it undeniably appears, 1. That the apostle apprehended these Hebrews to be in danger of total and final apostasy; 2. That he wrote this epistle to them on purpose to prevent it, if possible; and, 3. That of consequence it was total and final apostasy which he meant by neglecting this great salvation.

III. Thus having largely shewn what is meant by neglecting so great salvation, I proceed, Thirdly, to shew the consequence of neglecting it; together with the absolute impossibility of escaping that consequence, if we neglect it.

And, First, as to the consequence of neglecting it. This has often been mentioned in general, in the course of the preceding pages.

pages, But we will now be a little more particular.

In the verse preceding the text the apostle observes, that the word spoken by angels was stedfast, and that every transgression and disobedience received a JUST RECOMPENCE OF REWARD: that is, they received such a recompence as in its *quality* and *quantity*, was justly due to the *nature* and *degree* of such an offence. He then adds, "How shall we escape"—a just recompence of reward, "if we neg-"lect so great salvation?"—But what is that just recompence of reward which belongs to the neglecters of this salvation? I answer, such as in its *quality* and *quantity*, that is, in its NATURE and DEGREE is justly due to total and final apostasy.

As to the *nature* of the punishment, the apostle saith, chap. vi. verse 8. that "their END IS TO BE BURNED." Mr. *Henry*, on these words saith, "*Apostasy* will be punish-"ed with EVERLASTING BURNINGS, with "the fire that shall never be quenched. "This is the sad end to which *apostasy*
"leads,

" leads, and therefore Christians should go
" on, and grow in grace, lest if they do
" not go forward, they should go back-
" ward, till they bring matters to this wo-
" ful extremity of sin and misery*."

In chap. x. verse 27. we are informed with what they are to be burned, and also in what manner. And, first, they are to be burned with a *fiery indignation*. That is, with the fierce displeasure, wrath, and vengeance of a sin-avenging God. Secondly, this fiery indignation is to devour them. That is, it is to devour them, body and soul for ever. *Menochius* and *Estius*, as quoted by the calvinian *Pool*, say, " *Est*
" *prosopopœia, quâ igni tribuit vitam et*
" *vires, sensum, zelum pro gloria Dei, vindi-*
" *candisque illius injuriis, et impatientiam*
" *tantæ moræ et dilationis ; ut ignis sit in-*
" *star irritatæ feræ, quæ prædam apprehendit*
" *et devorat, vel instar lictoris acerbati, qui*
" *gestit vindicare :*" it is a prosopopœia, which attributes to fire, life, strength, sense, and zeal for God's glory, and for the re-
venging

* Henry on the place.

venging of the injuries done to him, and impatient of so long delay; insomuch that fire is represented like an angry wild beast, that seizes upon and devours its prey, or like an exasperated executioner who is impatient to strike the blow†. And *Estius* says again, "*Instar ignis acerrime et celerrime punit:*" like fire he punishes in the most quick and severe manner‖. Mr. *Henry* faith, "Some think this refers to the dreadful destruction of the Jewish church and state; but certainly it refers also to the utter destruction that awaits for all obstinate APOSTATES AT DEATH AND JUDGMENT, when the Judge shall discover a fiery indignation against them, that will devour the adversaries: *They will be consigned over to the devouring fire, and to everlasting burnings**." Thus the APOSTATES shall know, by woeful experience, that "Vengeance belongeth unto the Lord; that He will recompence; that He will judge the people; and that it is a dreadful thing for them

† Syn. Crit. in loc.　‖ Ibid.　* Henry on the place,

them to fall into the hands of the Living God," chap. x. verse 30, 31. and that to such, " Our God is a consuming fire." chap. xii. verse 29.

But in what *quantity*, or *degree* will this punishment be inflicted on them? I answer, It shall be inflicted in a larger quantity, or in a greater degree than upon any other sinners who ever lived.—To make this appear, I shall observe, 1. That the manifestations of Himself, which, from time to time, God has made to the world, have been in various degrees. The lowest manifestation of himself was to the Heathens, by the light of nature. The manifestation of himself made to the Jews, by *Moses* and the Prophets, rose several degrees higher. But the most clear, full, and perfect manifestation of all, is that made by *Christ* and his gospel: see chap. viii. verse 10, 11. chap. ix. verse 7—9. 11. Observe, 2. That as God has manifested himself to different people, in different degrees, so he will proportion their degrees of punishment to the measures of light and opportunity which they have received, and abused.

The Heathens, who abused the lowest dispensation of God's grace, will doubtless be very severely punished. So saith St. *Paul*. "Indignation and wrath, tribulation and anguish, to every soul of man that doeth evil; to the Jew first, and also the Greek," that is, the heathen who abused the light of nature. And that these will be severely punished, is evident from what God has already done in the case of some of them. *Jude* tells us that the people of "Sodom and Gomorrah are suffering the vengeance of eternal fire." Dreadful, then, is the punishment which God has already inflicted on the heathen world for neglecting, or abusing those inferior manifestations of his will. But as the revelation of his will, made by *Moses* and the prophets unto the Jews, is more great and glorious, so the punishment of such of them as are refractory and disobedient will be more great and terrible. So our Lord told the disobedient Jews of his day. " It shall be more tolerable for Sodom and Gomorrah in the day of Judgment than for you." As if he had said, Your punishment in kind shall be the same;

same; for you, with them, shall "suffer the vengeance of eternal fire." But as you have abused greater mercies, and sinned against greater light; your *degree* of that vengeance shall of consequence be greater. Our Lord then adds, "It shall be more tolerable for *Tyre* and *Sidon*, those other heathen cities, than for you. The men of *Nineveh*, also, and the queen of the South (all Heathens) shall rise up in judgment against this generation—of disobedient Jews, and shall condemn it." It is therefore certain, that severe as the punishment of disobedient heathens will be, that of disobedient Jews will be more severe and intolerable.

But how will it be with disobedient Christians? particularly, with those who so neglect this great salvation as to fall into total and final apostasy? I answer, their punishment shall be much greater than that of a disobedient Jew. The truth of this proposition is undeniable from chap. x. verse 28, 29, of this epistle. "He, said the apostle, that despised *Moses'* law, died

without mercy, under two or three witnesses: of HOW MUCH SORER punishment suppose ye, shall he be thought worthy, who hath trodden under foot the Son of GOD?" &c. Now, let it be well observed here, that the neglecter of this salvation, that the total and final apostate from Christ and his gospel, shall be counted worthy of (and, of consequence, receive) PUNISHMENT, SORER punishment, MUCH sorer than the rebellious and apostate Jews. So Bishop *Hopkins*, in his sermon on Heb. x 30, 31. "In the four precedent verses, we
"find the apostle threatening most tremendous judgments against all that
"should wilfully transgress, AFTER THEY
"HAD RECEIVED THE KNOWLEDGE OF
"THE TRUTH. He tells us, there remains
"no more sacrifice for their sins: nothing
"to expiate their guilt, but that THEY
"THEMSELVES MUST FALL a burnt sacri-
"fice to the offended justice of GOD, CON-
"SUMED with that FIERY INDIGNATION
"that shall CERTAINLY SEIZE and PREY
"on them FOR EVER. And in verse 28, 29.
"he

"he sets forth the exceeding dreadfulness
"of their judgment, by a comparison be-
"tween those that violate the law of *Moses*,
"and those that RENOUNCE and *annul* the
"law of *Christ*. He that despised Moses'
"law—was to die without mercy; cer-
"tainly much sorer judgments await those
"who reject the laws of *Christ*—such as
"these shall ETERNALLY PERISH with
"LESS MERCY, than those that died *with-
"out mercy**." So father *Quesnel*, "If
"there was no mercy for him who despised
"the law of Moses, in one single point;
"what ought the perjured person to ex-
"pect, who violates the Christian covenant,
"and tears off a member from *Jesus Christ*,
"by DESERTING HIM? Such a person
"will have both heaven and earth as wit-
"nesses against him, and GOD for a judge
"and avenger of his own cause‖." So on
ver. 30. "It belongs to GOD, to avenge the
"holiness of his covenant, when violated
"by APOSTASY and sin. Men punish as
"men:

* Bishop Hopkins's Works, 3d Edit. page 368.
‖ Quesnel's New Testament on the place.

"men. God punishes and executes ven-
"geance as God, that is, holily, infinitely,
"eternally§." It is therefore most infallibly certain, that the greatest measure,
the heaviest and most intolerable load of
the wrath of God, will be the consequence
of neglecting this great salvation.

Having shewn what the consequence of
neglecting it is, I proceed, Secondly, to
shew the *impossibility* of escaping this consequence if we neglect it. By IMPOSSIBILI-
TY of escaping I mean, that there is no way
of escaping which can possibly be found,
or means of it which can possibly be used.

But it may be said, " Does not the apos-
" tle suppose that there is some way or
" other to escape when he asks, how it may
" be done?" I answer, he supposes no
such thing. His words, properly understood, rather suppose the contrary. For,
when an impossibility is required, it is common to say, How can that be done? certainly the meaning is, it is impossible to do
it. And that this was the apostle's meaning

§ See Quesnel on the place.

ing in the passage under consideration, appears from chap. xii. verse 25. See that ye refuse not him that speaketh: for if they escaped not who refused him that spake on earth, *much more* SHALL NOT *we escape*, if we turn away from him that speaketh from heaven. Here then the apostle declares that WE SHALL NOT escape if we neglect this great salvation: that as it is certain, that those who refused him who spake on earth, DID NOT escape, so it is equally certain that we SHALL NOT escape, if we refuse him who speaketh from heaven. Mr. *Henry* on the place saith, " The misery " of such sinners is described, and declared " to be unavoidable, ver. 3. How shall " we escape? This intimates, 1. That the " despisers of this salvation are condemned, " under arrest, and in the hands of justice " already.—2. There is NO ESCAPING out " of this condemned state.—As for those " that neglect it, the wrath of God *is* upon " them, and it *abides* upon them, they " CANNOT DISENGAGE THEMSELVES, they " CANNOT emerge, they CANNOT get " from under the curse.—There is yet a more

"more aggravated curse and condemnation waiting for all those that despise the grace of God in *Christ*, and that *most heavy* curse they CANNOT ESCAPE— There is no door of mercy left open for them, there shall be no more sacrifice for sin, they are *irrecoverable*. The UN- AVOIDABLENESS of the misery of such is here expressed by way of question,— How shall we escape? It is an appeal to universal reason, to the consciences of sinners themselves; it is a challenge to all their power and policy, to all their interest and alliances, whether they, or any for them, can find out, or can force out, a way of escape from the vindictive justice and wrath of God†." Dr. *Owen* saith, that, "The design of the apostle in these verses is, to prove that they shall DESERVEDLY and ASSUREDLY PERISH who shall neglect the gospel§." Again, "The apostle in the next verses—lets them krow that their destruction IS CERTAIN, and that from God‖." And the reason why

---

† Henry on the place. § Owen on the place. ‖ Ibid.

why we shall not escape is, because it is impossible: God cannot in any wise, consistent with his wisdom, holiness, justice and truth, admit of it; for if he could possibly have done it, consistently with these attributes, there is no doubt but his goodness would have done it: therefore, I conclude, that there is no possibility of escaping for those who neglect this great salvation.

But it may be said, "Suppose I should "neglect this salvation, cannot I escape "by depending on the mercy of God?" I answer, No. For, though it be a great and sacred truth, that God is infinite in mercy, it will not follow—that the abusers of this mercy shall be saved thereby. St. *Paul* tells us, chap. x. verse 28. that "He that despised *Moses*' law *died* WITHOUT *mercy*, under two or three witnesses." He then adds, "Of *how much* SORER *punishment* suppose ye, shall he be thought worthy, who hath trodden under foot the Son of God," &c. As if he had said, The sin of despising Moses' law was so aggravated, that the mercy of God *would not* interpose in behalf of such an offender. Now, as the sin of those

those who have trodden under foot the Son of God, &c. is so much more heinous, there is abundantly more reason to believe that mercy will not interpose on their behalf; but rather that it will suffer the punishment they have so dearly deserved, to fall on them without remedy, and to remain on them for ever.

"But suppose I neglect this salvation, by totally and finally apostatizing, cannot I escape the afore-mentioned punishment, by living a sober, moral life?" I again answer, No. For the apostle declares, all over this epistle, that our salvation is by *Christ*, and by adhering unto him. So chap. 1. verse 3 *Christ* is said, by himself to have purged our sins: chap. ii. verse 9. to have tasted death for every man: verse 10. that he is the captain of our salvation: verse 14, 15. that he died to destroy the power of death—and to deliver them who through fear of death were all their life-time subject to bondage. verse 17. that he made reconciliation for the sins of the people: chap. iv. verse 14. that he is our great High Priest: verse 16. that he has erected a throne

throne of grace, unto which we are to come for mercy, &c. chap. v. verse 9. that he is become the author of eternal salvation unto all that obey him: chap. vi. verse 18. that he is our refuge to which we are to fly, that we may lay hold on the hope set before us: chap. viii. verse 6. that he is the Mediator of the new Covenant: chap. ix. verse 12. that he has obtained eternal redemption for us: verse 14. that it is his blood which purgeth our consciences from dead works to serve the living God: verse 15 that by his death we receive the promise of the eternal inheritance: verse 26. that he hath appeared to put away sin by the sacrifice of himself: chap. x. verse 5—9. that when God had no pleasure in Jewish sacrifices and offerings, a body was prepared for *Christ*, in which he freely and chearfully came to do the will of God: verse 10. by the which will we are sanctified, through the offering of the body of *Christ* once for all: verse 19. that we have boldness to enter into the holiest by the blood of *Jesus*: verse 38, that we live by faith in him: and

that

that thus it is, according to chap. 12. verse 2. that he is the author and finisher of our faith.

Now, from this account we learn, that the whole of our salvation, both in time and eternity, is by Christ and his gospel only: I say, *only*; for we are told, chap. 1. ver. 3 that Christ BY HIMSELF hath done it. And that our salvation is only by Christ, is so strongly implied, in almost every part of this epistle, that it cannot, with any shadow of reason, be denied. Therefore, I conclude, that whatever laws, or rules, a man may walk by, whether they be those delivered by Moses, or those laid down by Epictetus, Socrates, Seneca, or Plato; if he is a total and final apostate from this great salvation, he never can escape the dreadful consequence.

But it may be said once more, " Suppose " I should at present, or at any future " period thus neglect this great salvation, " will not my former attachment to it be " sufficient to screen me from the punish- " ment above mentioned?" I answer, it will not. And for proof of this I observe,
that

that, perhaps there never was a people more cordially, and zealously attached to Christ and his gospel, than these Hebrews had formerly been. For the apostle tells them, chap. x. verse 32,—34. that After they were illuminated, they endured a great fight of afflictions: partly, said he, whilst ye were made a gazing-stock, both by reproaches and afflictions; and partly whilst ye became companions of them that were so used. For ye had compassion of me in my bonds, and took joyfully the spoiling of your goods, knowing in yourselves that ye have in heaven a better and an enduring substance. On this passage I observe, that here was not only great zeal for Christ, his gospel and persecuted servant; but it was such as was built on a solid foundation: for they firmly adhered to Christ and the gospel for a while, and took joyfully the spoiling of their goods, " knowin themselves that in heaven they had a better and an enduring substance." And yet, notwithstanding all this, they are threatened with the sorest punishment that God has

to

to inflict, on suppofition that they apoftatize. It is therefore certain that paft attachments to Chrift, and zeal for his glory, be they never fo genuine and fervent, will not be fufficient to acquit thofe who fhall afterwards, by apoftafy, neglect this great falvation.

Having fhewn, I. What we are to underftand by fo great falvation: II. What by neglecting it. and, III. The confequence of fo doing, and the impoffibility of efcaping it; I now proceed in the IV. place to draw a few inferences from the whole.

1. And, Firft, from what has been faid we learn, that the doctrine of unconditional perfeverance is no truth of GOD; is no doctrine of revelation. This, the epiftle to the Hebrews moft abfolutely demonftrates. The total and final apoftafy of true believers, is the one fuppofition which runs through the whole epiftle, from beginning to end: and, as I have obferved above, the epiftle is no other than a regular treatife on this fubject, wherein every argument, proper on fuch an occafion, is ufed by the apoftle in the moft judicious, and conclufive

sive manner. Here then is solid proof that Christian believers are capable of TOTAL and FINAL *apostasy:* a whole book of the New Testament; which is justly deemed one of the most learned and excellent in all the sacred volume; drawn up into one argument, or rather into one chain of arguments, in support of the awful truth. To oppose such a CONNECTION of arguments with detached passages, picked up hither and thither, without any regard to the scope of the books, or the coherence of the places from whence they are taken, is a mode of reasoning so truly ridiculous, that it is astonishing how any man of real learning, or sober sense, can be capable of it.

If the doctrine of unconditional perseverance be a revealed truth, and if it be of such importance as the advocates for that doctrine continually assert, let them produce more certain evidence in its favour, than that which I have here produced against it. Or, if they cannot do this, let them produce an equal degree of evidence: that is, let them

them point out a whole book of the New Testament, of equal dignity and importance with this epistle to the Hebrews, which labours, as professedly and fully, in support of their hypothesis. Or if this is too much, let them produce a canonical book of less importance, which thus professedly and logically supports it. But this cannot be done: no whole book; no half book; no, nor so much as the quarter of any one book in all the bible, can be pointed out which maintains this doctrine in a regular succession of conclusive arguments.—No other proof of it can be given, than that which depends on the sound of tortured words, draged into the service, without any regard to the connexion of the places from whence they are taken; and therefore it is impossible, without the most palpable absurdity, to suppose that it is any doctrine of Revelation; or that it is any other than one of those divers and strange doctrines, mentioned chap. xiii. verse 9. by which we are not to be carried about.

And from hence we learn that the doctrine

trine of unconditional election is no truth of Revelation. This doctrine supposes that God hath, from eternity, unconditionally elected, or chosen, a certain number unto eternal life. That, in order to this end, they were absolutely decreed to be born in time, to be called by the gospel; to obey the call; to be converted thereby; and to persevere to the end. Now, if it can be demonstrated that these persons have failed in ANY of these particulars, this will equally demonstrate that they were not thus unconditionally elected. For instance: if we can demonstrate that these supposed persons were not actually born in time, this will demonstrate that they were not elected to that end, and by those means above mentioned; seeing that one of these means, and that which is indispensably necessary, in order to the existence and use of the rest, never existed. Or suppose they were born in time, yet if it can be fairly proved that they were never called and converted by the gospel, this will prove that they were not thus elected to everlasting life; seeing that those intermediate means, which the supposed decree has made equally necessary with that before mentioned, never existed. But if we allow them to be born, and also, to be called and converted by the gospel, yet if they did not persevere to the end, but fell away and perished for ever, it is most infallibly certain that they were not unconditionally elected to everlasting life, seeing it is not possible that GOD should thus elect them to it, and that after all they should not enjoy it. But it has been demonstrated, in the preceding pages, that persons born in time, and called and converted by the gospel, may nevertheless fall away and perish for ever; and therefore I conclude that such persons were not unconditionally elected unto everlasting life: and, of consequence, that the doctrine which supposes the contrary is no truth of Revelation.

And from hence we learn farther, that the doctrine which asserts that all things are unconditionally decreed from eternity is no truth of Revelation. This doctrine supposes that every cause, and every effect, that every event and circumstance attending it, which did,

did, does, or shall exist, was most absolutely, unconditionally, and unchangeably decreed from eternity: that this is particularly the case in the decree of election, where every circumstance attending the salvation of the elect, such as their birth, calling, conversion and perseverance were all unconditionally decreed from everlasting: God has unconditionally decreed whatever exists; but in the execution of the decree of election, the perseverance of true believers exists; therefore, God has unconditionally decreed it. To this I answer, it has been demonstrated, in the preceding pages, that the perseverance of true believers does not always infallibly exist; yea, that it never exists unconditionally: seeing they may, yea, and often do, fall away and perish for ever. I therefore conclude, First, that the perseverance of the saints is not unconditionally decreed: that of consequence, Secondly, all things cannot be thus decreed: and that therefore, Thirdly, the doctrine which supposes the unconditional decree of all things, is no truth of Revelation.

Inference 2. From what has been said we learn, Secondly, that christian-believers ought to be careful not to neglect this great salvation. Doubtless it was a conviction of the need and importance of this care, which caused the apostle to lay down the weighty cautions, solemn warnings, and awful admonitions which we find all over this epistle; and doubtless a like conviction ought to awaken all to whom these cautions belong, to receive them in a becoming manner. Now as we, and all christian-believers, at all times, and in all places, are in danger of neglecting this salvation, are in danger of total and final apostasy, it highly behoves us to suffer ourselves to be admonished.

Let us then, one and all, take earnest heed to the things, of Christ, which we have heard, lest at any time we should, *by apostasy*, let them slip out of our hearts, lips and lives, chap. ii. verse 1. Let us, instead of *apostatizing*, hold fast the confidence, and the rejoicing of the hope, firm unto the end of our lives, chap. iii. verse 6. Let us, on no account, nor by any means, harden our hearts

as in the provocation, in the day of temptation in the wildernefs, verfe 8. Let us take earneft heed left there be in any of us an evil heart of unbelief in *departing, totally* and *finally*, from Chrift, who is the living God, verfe 12. Let us, from the confideration of the danger of *apoftafy* which we are all in, exhort one another daily, while it is called, To-day; left any of us be fo hardened through the deceitfulnefs of fin, as to *apoftatize from Chrift*, and his falvation, verfe 13. Let us ferioufly, deeply, and conftantly fear, left a promife being left us of entering into his reft, any of us, by *apoftatizing*, fhould come fhort of it, chap. iv. verfe 1. Let us rather labour, with all our might, to enter into that reft, left any man *fall*, totally and finally, after the fame example of unbelief, or difobedience, which was found among the Ifraelites of old, verfe 11. Let us couragioufly, and in oppofition to all the powers of darknefs, *hold faft* our Chriftian profeffion, verfe 14. Let us, inftead of *apoftatizing from,* come boldly *unto* the throne of grace, that we may obtain pardoning mercy for what is paft, and
find

find grace, *persevering* grace, to help us in every future time of need, verse 16. Instead of *apostatizing* from that measure of the Christian life which we now enjoy, let us rather go on unto perfection, chap. vi. verse 1. Let us shew the same diligence, which we have formerly shewn, to the full assurance of hope *unto the end of our lives,* verse 11. Let us not be slothful, in cleaving to, and obeying Christ; but rather be followers of them, who, in spite of all opposition, through *stedfast* faith, and *unwearied* patience, inherit the promises, verse 12. Let us *continue* to draw near to God with a true heart, in full assurance of *persevering* faith in Jesus, chap. x. verse 22. Let us *hold fast* the open profession of our faith without *wavering* any longer, verse 23. Let us consider one another, how weak we are, and how liable to *grow weary* of the cross of Christ; and therefore let us study how we may provoke each other unto love and to good works, verse 24. Let us not *forsake* the assembling of ourselves together, as the manner of some is, who have already *apostatized*; but let us rather exhort

hort one another, to *conſtancy* and *perſeverance;* and ſo much the more, as we ſee the day of heavier trial ſwiftly approaching, verſe 25. Let us not ſin wilfully, by *total* and *final apoſtaſy*, after we have truly, and experimentally, received the ſaving knowledge of the goſpel-truth, verſe 26. Let us rather call to our remembrance the former days, in which, after we were ſpiritually illuminated, we couragiouſly *endured* a great fight of afflictions, verſe 32. and let this encourage us, inſtead of *apoſtatizing*, to endure, in the ſame manner, whatever may befal us in time to come. Let us not *caſt away* our holy confidence, which hath great recompence of reward, verſe 35. Let us lay aſide every weight, and the ſin which doth ſo eaſily beſet us, and let us continue to run with *patient perſeverance* the race that is ſet before us, chap. xii. verſe 1. Let us be ever looking to the holy example of Jeſus, who is the author and finiſher of our faith; who for the joy that was ſet before him, *patiently* and *perſeveringly endured* the croſs, deſpiſing the ſhame, and is

ſet

set down at the right hand of the throne of God, verse 2. Let us consider the example of him, who *stedfastly*, and to the very *last moment* of his life, *endured* the contradiction of sinners against himself, lest we be *wearied* and *faint* in our mind, and so *apostatize* from Christ and his gospel, verse 3. Let us manfully *endure* the chastning of the Lord, nor *faint* when we are rebuked of him, verse 5. That the feeblest soul among us may not *apostatize*, let us lift up the hands which hang down, and the feeble knees, verse 12. Let us make straight paths for the feet of each other, lest that which is lame be turned out of the way of Christ, into *apostasy*, verse 13. Instead of *backsliding*, let us follow peace with all men, and holiness, without which no man shall see the Lord, verse 14. Let us look diligently, lest any man *fall from* the grace of God; lest any root of bitterness, that is, any backslider, or apostate, springing up, trouble us, and thereby many others be defiled, verse 15. Let us not refuse, or *turn away from him*, (that is, from Christ) that
speaketh

speaketh from heaven, verse 25. Let us *hold fast* the grace we have, whereby we may continue to serve God acceptably, with reverence and godly fear, verse 28. Let brotherly love *continue to the end.* chap. xiii. verse 1. And instead of *leaving the gospel,* and associating ourselves with unconverted Jews, let us not be forgetful to entertain Christian strangers, verse 2. Let us remember them that are in bonds for Christ and his gospel, as if we were bound with them, verse 3. Let our conversation be without covetousness; and let us, for Christ's sake, be content with such things as we have, verse 5. Let us not be *carried away* with the divers and strange doctrines, taught by the Gnosticks, and other heretics; and particularly that doctrine which teaches that true believers cannot fall away totally and finally, verse 9. Let us go forth *unto* (not *from*) Jesus without the camp, *patiently,* and *stedfastly* bearing his reproach, verse 13. Instead of *forsaking Christ,* by him let us offer the sacrifice of praise to God *continually,* verse 15. To do good and to com-

communicate, let us not forget, or *grow weary*; seeing that with such sacrifices God is well pleased, verse 16. Let each of you obey them that have the rule over you, and submit yourselves: for they watch over your souls, that you may not *depart from Christ* into *apostasy*, as they that must give account, verse 17. Pray for them, that God may preserve *them* from *apostasy*, and that he may make them the happy instruments of *preserving all those* committed to their care, verse 18.

Thus, upon the whole, let you and I, and all who desire to be preserved from total and final apostasy, suffer the word of exhortation, verse 22. Let the consideration of the *superior excellency* of Christ's person and religion; of the *dreadful punishment* which will certainly be inflicted on all who *apostatize* from them; of the *great reward* which will be given to all who *persevere* to the end; of the great *loss of past labours* and *present privileges* which *apostates* shall infallibly sustain; and of the *dishonour* of acting a part so exceeding contrary to the
example

example of all the antient worthies, which have been since the world began: I say, let all these solemn considerations stir us up to *cleave* to Jesus with our whole heart; to follow him closely, and *stedfastly*, in all the ways of Christian obedience, till we are called to enjoy that Rest which remains for the people of God, chap. iv. verse 9.

Now the God of Peace that brought again from the dead our Lord Jesus, that great Shepherd of the sheep, through the blood of the everlasting covenant, make you perfect in every good work to do his will, working in you all, that wisdom, holiness, happiness and *perseverance,* which is well-pleasing in his sight, through Jesus Christ; to whom be glory for ever and ever. Amen. Chap. xiii. verse 20, 21.

FINIS.

BOOKS
WRITTEN AND PUBLISHED
BY
The AUTHOR.

                                              Price

I. A Hymn on the Last Judgment, set to Music by the Author, The 20th edit.   3d

II. A Hymn of Praise to Christ, set to Music by a Gentleman in Ireland, and performed before the late Bishop of Waterford, in his Cathedral, on Christmas-Day, 3d edition. To which is added a Hymn on Matt. v. 29, 30. The second edition.   1s

III. A Hymn to the God of Abraham, adapted to a celebrated air, sung by Mr. Leoni, in the Jews Synagogue, London. The 30th edition.   1d

IV. A Letter to Mr. Thomas Hanby, occasioned by the sudden death of several near Relations.   1d

V. Twelve

Price

V. Twelve Reasons why the people called Methodists ought not to buy or sell uncustomed goods. —— 1d

VI. An Answer to a Pamphlet, entitled, A few Thoughts and Matters of Fact concerning Methodism, offered to the consideration of the people, who attend, encourage, and support Methodist Teachers. In a Letter to the Author. —— —— 1d

VII. A full Reply to a Pamphlet, entitled, An Answer to a late Pamphlet of Mr. Wesley against Mr Erskine, 3d

VIII. A Letter to the Rev. Mr. Toplady, occasioned by his late Letter to the Rev. John Wesley. —— 4d

IX. A Scourge to Calumny, in two Parts, Inscribed to Richard Hill, Esq. Part the first, Demonstrating the absurdity of that Gentleman's Farrago. Part the second, Containing a full Answer to all that is material in his Farrago Double distilled. —— 1s 6d

X. A full Defence of the Rev. John Wesley, in answer to the several personal Reflections cast on that Gentleman, by the Rev. Caleb Evans. —— 2d

XI. A

Price

XI. A Rod to a Reviler: or an Answer to the Rev. Rowland Hill's Letter to the Rev. John Wesley, — 6d

XII. A Defence of Methodism: Delivered ex tempore in a public debate, (but now considerably enlarged) held in London, December 12, 19, and 26, 1785. on the following question, Have the Methodists done most good or evil? 4d

XIII. A full Refutation of the doctrine of unconditional perseverance; in a discourse on Hebrews, chap. ii. verse 3. In which the possibility and danger of the total and final apostasy of true believers is demonstrated: and the epistle to the Hebrews is shewn to be no other than a regular Treatise, or one connected chain of reasoning, on that subject. 2s 6d

XIV. A short Account of the Life of Mr. Thomas Olivers, — — 6d

CPSIA information can be obtained
at www.ICGtesting.com
Printed in the USA
BVHW01s1411040518
515322BV00011B/304/P